Remember the Roses

BY
LYNETTE LEWIS

Dear Kerri,
Your Story HIS
Glory!
Lynette

Published by Carpenter's Son Publishing, Franklin, Tennessee

Published in association with Larry Carpenter of Christian Book Services, LLC
www.christianbookservices.com

Cover and Interior Layout Design: Suzanne Lawing

Illustrations: Deborah Coates

Printed in the United States of America

978-0-9849771-4-7

I prayed for one man to love, and got five.

This book is dedicated to my incredible husband, Ron Lewis, and our four sons, Nathan, Christian, Jordan, and Johnluke.

Every day you remind me that holding out for the BEST is worth it all.

Table of Contents

To enjoy photos of people and events in *Remember the Roses*, visit LynetteLewis.com and the Lynette Lewis Page on Facebook.

Acknowledgments

This story includes so many who helped me endure, thrive, and make it to the finish line.

My husband, **Ron Lewis.** This is *our* story; thank you for letting me share it. You continue to exceed all expectations and make every day a fun, exciting adventure.

My parents, **Howard and Geneva Troyer.** Your marriage of 54 years sets the bar for my own. Your untiring love, faith, and support have held me every step of the way.

My sister, **Brenda Hendryx.** Lifelong playmate, confidant, prayer partner, best friend. Barbie and Ken have nothing on us! I love you forever, my sissy.

Kim Ford, Toni Fowler, Kathi Graves, Judi Kohlbacher. Bridesmaids, best friends, women I want to be like in every way. Thank you for never giving up and always saying yes.

Sue Behr and Chene' Tucker. Your prayers availed. Your stories are not over yet.

Pete, Mary Kay, and the Bible study gang. We stood together til faith became sight. The "demon of diamonds" may live on, but so do our friendships across the miles.

Paul Shepherd, literary agent. Thank you for believing in this story from the beginning. You are a true professional and man of excellence.

God my Savior. For making dreams come true, exceedingly over and above all I imagined. Eternity with you will be the ultimate True Love reward.

Introduction

Have you noticed the mixed messages lately? Popular media telling us love, sex, and romance are the ultimate high, while applauding a lifestyle of casual sex and living together that often destroys intimacy and fulfillment.

Against this backdrop I share my story. Not as the end-all/be-all, but as one modern-day example of principles that produce joy and fulfillment for hundreds of people I know.

Not everyone will resonate with this journey, but I am passionate about offering it as an alternative to so many sad examples today. My intent is to be honest and real so that you, too, will wait as long as it takes for the relationship of your dreams.

Mine is a story of waiting -- that rigorous, sometimes messy, often frustrating, process of waiting. It is also a story of dreams coming true, because no matter how long it takes, God is faithful and He does answer prayers.

This story is told in three sections: the first details the journey leading up to and through our wedding. The second highlights gifts received and lessons learned (most not understood until later). Finally, a handful of journal excerpts illustrate common emotions rarely discussed publicly, but those so often present when love tarries.

Since pictures are worth a thousand words, I have posted many photos that complement each chapter. You can enjoy these by visiting www.LynetteLewis.com.

Most of all...welcome to a growing community of visionaries worldwide, those of us choosing to *Remember the Roses* on the sometimes rocky pathway to finding love and living our dreams.

The Road with the Roses

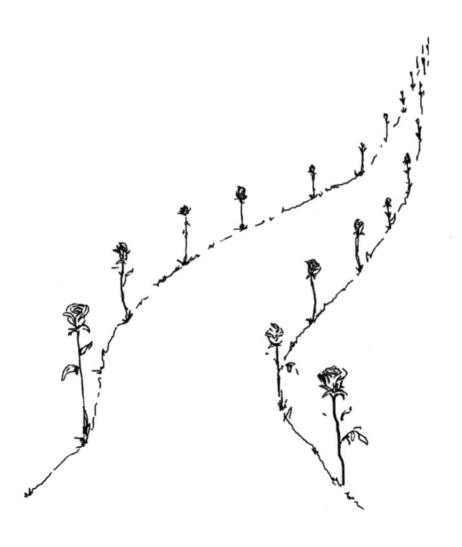

CHAPTER 1

Barbie Was Married

Virtually every woman I know dreams of love and marriage. Wedding magazines sell by the thousands—both to those getting married and not.

Being single in a doubles world can often feel lonely, but in reality there are millions of singles; in fact, there are nearly 100 million unmarried people over age 18 in the United States alone.[1]

For as long as I can remember, my own dreams for a husband, children, and a home filled with laughter and love, grew in my heart and mind. I felt certain these dreams would come true by age 25, never expecting to turn 40 and still be waiting.

Growing up in Indiana, the oldest of two daughters, I expressed my dreams through Barbie, Ken and the "Barbie Universe" my sister, Brenda, and I created in our basement. We had the "Dream Houses" that folded down from the back, with cars, campers, and wardrobes to envy.

My Barbie had blonde hair like mine, and Brenda's had brown

like hers. The Kens were identical, so our story of their lives was that identical twin brothers married fraternal twin sisters and each couple had one daughter, Skipper (mine) and Leisha (Brenda's.) We played for hours on end, and through their lives envisioned our own joyful futures.

Being in the so-called "popular group" in high school did not guarantee a boyfriend or a date. Friends and I went to school dances and danced together in groups, hoping no one noticed we were envying the few dancing with the guys.

> The prom picture came back showing the two of us, slightly smiling, his arms awkwardly posed around mine—and his eyes completely closed!

I never attended our high school proms, though I was invited by a family friend to a prom at another school. Decked out in the perfect dress, with a nervous stomach off I went. The prom picture came back showing the two of us, slightly smiling, his arms awkwardly posed around mine—and his eyes completely closed!

How well that seemed to portray what it felt like during the teenage years – like every guy had his eyes shut. My Mom, always the encourager and woman of faith, said it was God protecting me from bad situations, that He had put a veil on their eyes so I would not be misused or make regrettable mistakes. I remember thinking: *Thanks Mom, I hope it is true, but when will I be the object of affection?*

At age 18 it was off to Tulsa, Oklahoma, to attend Oral Roberts University, a Christian liberal arts school of about 4,000 students, most of whom live on campus. With 2,000 men and 2,000 women, this must mean, "There is one for every one! Surely this fertile field of available men will yield a girl a husband."

Freshman year felt like one big party, though not in the typical college sense of carousing or drunkenness, since most of us at ORU found other means for fun.

The campus had a brilliant concept called "brother/sister wings," our homestyle version of the Greek system. Every girl's floor in the dorm was paired with a guy's floor. You ate with your brother wing, hung out on weekends, and developed quality, lasting relationships. Still, amidst all the fun and dates that year, none clicked.

Meanwhile, my roommate and dear friend, Diana, paired up with John Mark from the brother wing. They, along with four other couples from our floors, got engaged our freshman year. It seemed easy for everyone else to find the perfect mate, but certainly not for me.

Throughout those college years, while many were meeting the men of their dreams, my vision for a husband grew. I spent hours envisioning the qualities and characteristics I desired, praying about traits most essential for a life partner.

> I had a dream while sleeping, one that would go on to be a hallmark vision in my life; it was a dream full of hope, truths, and roses.

During my sophomore year, at a time I was especially longing for a husband to be revealed, I had a dream while sleeping, one that would go on to be a hallmark vision in my life; it was a dream full of hope, truths, and roses.

I was returning to the dorm in between classes and decided to take a nap. Not typically a napper, I had started taking short breaks in the afternoons, preparing for late-night studying ahead.

On this day, in the dream, I saw a woman walking slowly and determinedly along a brick road. The road twisted and turned as it went along, with single, long-stemmed roses planted about a yard apart on each side.

The woman kept walking along, seeming not to notice the roses planted there. Her eyes were fixed straight ahead, enamored with what she saw at the end of the road.

From time to time men would come up to the road, pick a rose, and hand it to her, but she would never take the roses they offered. Instead, she kept her gaze fixed firmly on what was ahead.

After she had walked for a while, another road—looking quite similar to hers—began to emerge in the picture. There was a man walking on that road, his gait much like hers and his eyes equally fixed on the end of the road. In his arm was the most beautiful bouquet of roses I had ever seen.

Before long the two roads became one and as they did, he reached out and took her hand, presenting her with the bouquet from his other hand. Neither turned to look at each other, but they remained transfixed on the end, now walking hand in hand.

Their walk eventually took them into the most magnificent garden, full of every imaginable flower, fragrant and so alive. What struck me most about this garden was the obvious presence of the Lord.

As they stood before Him, His glory now streaming down upon their faces, I heard His voice say to them, *"Well done, good and faithful servants. Enter into the glorious garden of reward I've prepared for you."*

I awoke from this dream a bit groggy, barely remembering the details, but over the next few days, writing in my journal, it came back with greater clarity. I asked God if there was a deeper meaning to this unusual dream. Here is what I sensed Him saying…

Lynette, I have called you to a road of my choosing and I want you to keep your eyes on me. At times along this path there will come men who have good things to offer, but I want you to keep your eyes only on me. For at the proper time of my choosing, I will bring to you a man who has walked a similar road, and who, like you, has his eyes transfixed on me. When he comes into your life he will not distract you, but rather he will strengthen you. He will have ALL the qualities your heart desires, and the two of you will walk together through the remainder of your lives. When you finish and stand before me, I will tell you, "I am well pleased." Then you will enter into my glory, a glory I am preparing even now for you.

Wow, what a powerful, truth-filled dream. Little did I know how often I would need this dream in the years to come, or how many others would embrace it as their own.

---

[1] U.S. Census Bureau, "America's Families and Living Arrangements: 2010"

CONSIDER THESE QUESTIONS

As a young girl, how did you think it would look in your future relative to marriage and family?

What has been the biggest "surprise" as you have walked your journey?

How do you resonate with Lynette's vision of The Road with the Roses?

CHAPTER 2

Brokenness Is a Pain

Junior year of college I was a resident advisor (RA), a position I embraced wholeheartedly, leading the women on the floor.

I was fighting discouragement about my weight at the time, having put on the "Freshmen 10," which before long became 20 unwanted pounds.

At the same time running became a favorite fitness routine. Perhaps some of the weight gain was due to muscle, but clothes did not fit and the weight was not dropping. Discouragement and a growing sense of failure prevailed.

Being an RA was fulfilling, but for some reason it also seemed like one pressure too many. This responsibility, along with the weight gain and other college pressures, began to take a toll on my emotional well-being.

I was in tears much of the time with an increasing sense of not coping. It felt like a strong pressure constantly in place -- the pressure to be excellent and perfect, what all the girls on the floor needed, a great student, a great friend, the right kind of faithful daughter and sister, be this and be that. It felt like the world was pressing in all around; the weight gain only compounded the despair.

My parents were a source of counsel on numerous occasions, sorting out what was happening and why I could not seem to cope. They wisely suggested counseling. Our family knew the benefits of counseling as my parents had gone early in their marriage and received tremendous tools and help from it.

> It felt like a strong pressure constantly in place -- the pressure to be excellent and perfect.

A dear friend offered her apartment as a temporary getaway, while at the same time I began meeting with a counselor on campus. Over the next six weeks the counselor helped peel away the layers, getting to the root issues of the pain.

He asked about my parents and upbringing. I considered my parents role models, nearly perfect in their parenting, our home always stable and a favorite place to be. I had not recognized that a crucial element was missing from my emotional development.

Dad was a faithful man, having served the Lord all his life, a true man of character, our "Steady Eddie" in a house of three women. What Dad was not, was an expressive man.

There were no memories of him expressing verbal love or showing physical affection. I had not recognized the lack since cognitively I knew he loved us. Mom told us how proud Dad was of his girls, and we spent time together as a family.

The counselor helped bring to light the lack of emotional and physical nurturing, resulting in my compensating attempts to be perfect. "When I am finally perfect enough," I subconsciously reasoned, "Dad will finally say 'I love you' and express his pride."

Becoming an RA added one thing too many to be perfect in, the one thing forcing deeper issues to the surface. What I was crying out for, and needing desperately, was my father's approval. It was time to finally acknowledge a legitimate void existed.

In a society where brokenness abounds, virtually everyone, on some level, has a father wound. According to James L. Schaller, MD, this unhealed wound has left many people "with a void, an injury, a psychic thirst that only a father can quench (that)... is nearly universal."[2]

Anyone who has gone through effective counseling knows that coming to the truth brings a freedom like never before. Suddenly so much made sense.

I learned to recognize patterns of striving for perfection and the toll they took on me and others. When the performance factor would kick in I would stop and realize I was operating with wrong motives.

I turned to the Lord for the healing so needed, spending time in prayer and reading the Bible. I meditated on Scriptures that talk about how we are loved and chosen by God, that His affections run deep, that He knows the number of hairs on our head and has written us into the palm of His hand. My journals became filled with God's words of affection, those I longed to hear from Dad.

> Anyone who has gone through effective counseling knows that coming to the truth brings a freedom like never before.

Slowly but surely a new freedom and joy emerged. I looked to God as the only source of affirmation that will ever truly satisfy. I focused on developing healthy male and female friendships as well.

In spite of these issues, my relationship with my Dad has always been good. After the season of healing, it was even better. He did not change all that much, but I changed.

By taking responsibility for what was broken, and not blaming others, I was, in essence, rewriting the script. Armed with the tools of counseling, I could help others do the same.

Thus began an exciting journey of acknowledging pain, then seeking healing and wholeness from the One true Healer. I made a lifelong commitment to refuse substitutions, seeking only for the Truth that will set us free and keep us free to be our true, healthy selves.

> By taking responsibility for what was broken, and not blaming others, in essence, I was rewriting the script.

Perhaps you recognize brokenness in your own life and if so, join the crowd! I have yet to meet one person who does not need healing in some way. Oprah Winfrey echoed this on her final episode, saying, "When I started this show it was a revelation to all of us how much dysfunction there is in people's lives."[3]

Pride keeps us from admitting it, while distractions keep us from addressing it. Wounds bring brokenness, which lead to dysfunction and bad habits. Rather than choosing "healed and happy," we accept "broken and disappointed."

Fortunately, healing is available for anyone who wants it. And if true love is in your future, believe me, you want it!

---

[2] James L. Schaller, MD, *The Search for Lost Fathering*, (Grand Rapids: Fleming H. Revell, 1995), Chapter 1: "Everybody Needs a Father."

[3] "The Oprah Winfrey Show Finale." The Oprah Winfrey Show. Prod. Harpo Productions Inc. ABC. WABC, New York. 25 May 2011.

CONSIDER THESE QUESTIONS

What areas of brokenness have you recognized in your own life, especially related to relationships?

Have you begun addressing these issues?

If not, why? If so what has your path toward healing involved?

CHAPTER 3

Dates and Heartbreak

Nearing graduation from college, my Grandma told me she had decided what would be my wedding gift someday -- a gorgeous set of antique English rose china, 12 of everything: plates, big and little bowls, cups, saucers, serving pieces. It had been a gift to her from a dying friend.

What a perfect selection for one who so loves to entertain! She said I could take it now, while moving into my own apartment, or wait until I was married. "Dear Grandma," I said, "you of all people know I'll be getting married any day now. So why not take it now and put it to use, versus waiting for my busy wedding season?"

Use it I did...for dozens of bridal showers, baby showers, birthday parties, and brunches, and on mornings when I needed my coffee in an extra special cup. Wedding china -- a treasured gift -- awaiting a wedding for more than 20 years.

Graduation Day arrived and all of my bridesmaids were selected. But alas, no husband in sight. I decided to take an optimistic view

– "Living on my own will surely be a value-add preparation for the awesome man with the roses."

Television degree in hand, I wondered if I could be the next Barbara Walters. Yes perhaps, but paying the bills was a strong incentive, so the first three years I worked for a personnel placement agency, recruiting people for temp jobs.

This first work experience was stimulating, meeting new people in the community and honing professional skills. "I will have a career for a few years," I reasoned, "and any day now my gifted husband will come. He will have a successful business career and by 25, we will start a family."

> Graduation Day arrived and all of my bridesmaids were selected. But alas, no husband in sight.

One day on a plane for business, I saw a handsome, red-haired man walking to his seat. A few weeks later, at a work event with my colleague Kathy, the very same guy walked by.

"Now *he* could be my type," I casually told her. Amazingly, she knew him, quite well in fact. She introduced us a few days later.

Over the next several months we began dating and to my delight he also was a graduate of ORU. Our relationship grew. I had my first kiss at the age of 25.

He was working through issues related to his first marriage that, although short-lived, had left him wounded and afraid. Nonetheless, my feelings grew, as did the conviction that *Surely I've waited all these years for this man. I can be a vessel of healing in his life.*

Sadly, what began as an exciting, hope-filled relationship started hitting up against his unresolved issues. We took things too far physically; I retained my virginity but crossed boundaries I had no peace in crossing.

The excitement of this first serious relationship turned into deep disappointment. I cried more tears than I ever thought possible, lost the weight, but now looked sickly. Hope deferred does indeed make the heart sick, and a sick heart can often be seen in a sickly looking body.

After about 10 months there was clearly a need to move on, and so we did. The dream for a husband remained unfulfilled, and my heart felt broken into a hundred different pieces.

> I cried more tears than I ever thought possible…hope deferred does indeed make the heart sick.

Meanwhile my best friend, Toni, met and married David. Within the first year she got pregnant and had her first son. Virtually every two years going forward, she would have another child, each one a precious gift to enjoy alongside Toni and David.

We had a sweet tradition on Sunday nights, sitting around the family table. I had the kids over for sleepovers, experiencing vicarious motherhood while waiting for my own. When would it ever come?

In those early years after graduation, I got involved with a wonderful Bible study group that included both guys and girls. We met each week on Friday nights at Pete and Mary Kay's home. Of the entire group, only two couples were married. The rest of us were single, about 15 in all. We experienced the joy of committed, heart-to-heart friendships, staying late after each study, laughing, talking, walking through life together.

Over the next few years several began meeting their spouses and getting engaged. The real test was how well the new person would fit in with the group, and gratefully, each one did. Lisa and I remained single the longest and chose to make light of it on several occasions.

At one of our group's annual Christmas parties we performed our own rendition of a Christmas classic, our version entitled "I'm Dreaming of a White Christian," (Obviously, this was a play on words, but it did not reflect any ethnic preference whatsoever.)

Donned in our beautiful Christmas dresses, we arose from the table, proceeded up to the front of the room, and began serenading our friends to the tune of the classic carol, "White Christmas"….

"I'm dreaming of a white Christian,
Just like the ones I've never known.
With big, bright eyes,
That tell me no lies,
And teeth that sparkle like the snow.
I'm dreaming of a white Christian
With every prophecy I write.
We will have great romance each night.
Here I stand by faith, not sight."

Our friends cheered and everyone laughed and laughed. Lisa and I left the stage saying, "Our phrase for this coming year is, 'We won't wait past '88.'"

Thus began our annual tradition of a phrase that captured ongoing wishes for marriage. *Men and Wine in '89! Falling Behind-y in 1990. Find the One in '91.* The phrases ceased when Lisa went on to meet and marry Sean. Tim married Sandy. Danny married Carrie. Hal was dating Gayle.

It was about this time that a fellow group member and close friend, Joel, and I began to consider a relationship with each other. Our friends liked the idea. We felt no red lights, so we started dating.

Things were exciting and went great for a while. They crumbled after about nine months. He thought I expected too much. I thought he was too immature. The relationship ended, and did it ever do a number to the heretofore-nicely-cohesive group.

It was awkward now for everyone. I was disappointed and sad. He was too, but covered it over better than I did.

Shortly after our breakup he started dating Kirsten, eight years his junior (which, of course, I credited to his immaturity). They got serious right away, which only dug a dagger deeper into my heart.

After they had been dating a number of months, a West Coast friend introduced me to a guy in Los Angeles. We began a long-distance relationship writing letters and enjoying phone calls.

Our in-person introduction finally happened, and boy did the sparks fly! Surely this was why the previous relationships had not succeeded. *This is the man for me!*

After three months, feeling certain we had a future together, plans were made to go meet my family in Indiana for Thanksgiving.

At the beginning of November an all-too-familiar dynamic started emerging. He expressed the need to slow down, to give it more time. A week before Thanksgiving, a letter arrived saying he needed to get out of the relationship. "Please don't call me as I'm not ready to talk about it yet," he wrote. Despair beyond words flooded my soul.

I flew home to Indiana alone, devastated, while back in Tulsa friends were all attending Joel and Kirsten's wedding. Two weeks later, Gayle called to say she and Hal were engaged.

Sitting by my parents' bed sobbing from the depths of my gut and soul, it was pain on a whole new level. Pain from dreams unfulfilled; agony over prayers not answered and what that must mean about God. Either He was all-powerful and simply did not care, or He was not that powerful at all.

Both ideas brought a new level of anguish and pain. No one seemed to relate to these emotions. It seemed like few, if any, faced this kind of loneliness and despair.

That night and in the years that followed, now in my early thirties, I was crying out to God with frequent emotion, wrestling for answers. Other than the few issues with my Dad, life had been quite golden. So what went wrong?

> Why must I still wait, God? Isn't it time for the two roads to come together? What must I do to convince you I am ready?

Why must I still wait, God? Isn't it time for the two roads to come together? What must I do to convince you I am ready? Are you so busy with everyone else's dreams you have forgotten about me? Numerous times in college I had felt the Lord prompting me to fast and pray for my husband. Had these prayers simply fallen on deaf ears?

All this wrestling flew in the face of my theology, a theology perhaps untested and naïve. Yes, God is a good God. He longs to be gracious to us. If we have faith as small as a grain of mustard seed He will move on our behalf. Ask and it will be given. He will give us the desires of our heart.

But equally true is the fact there will be suffering; there will be pain we do not understand or deserve. Prayers and questions may go unanswered for years. It is at these all-important junctures that we will choose to bail or to believe.

Will we draw our own conclusions about God in a vacuum, using our own experience as a barometer of His faithfulness and character? Or alternatively, will we humble ourselves, submit to the testings and trials, admit weaknesses, and seek knowledge from others more mature?

In the Bible, every servant of God suffers, some physically, others emotionally. Hebrews 11 speaks of the great men and women of faith who faced all types of sufferings, including being sawed in two!

Though everything inside us resists it, God often turns these painful experiences into gifts -- surprise gifts we would not choose for ourselves, but gifts we nonetheless need.

> Would I embrace the process and go to a deeper level of maturity and compassion, or abandon it altogether, and become increasingly bitter?

In these moments of desperation we become desperate for our One True Love, the One who faithfully meets us, though not always in the timing or way we would prefer.

When despondency and discouragement sought to overtake my heart and soul, I would face a crucial choice, not just once, but many times. Would I embrace the process and go to a deeper level of maturity and compassion, or abandon it altogether, and become increasingly bitter?

"I want to go deeper and remember the roses," I decided. "Even if it feels crazy, without an ounce of faith left to believe."

CONSIDER THESE QUESTIONS

What has your dating life looked like?

How have you dealt with heartbreaks?

Have you ever wrestled with or struggled with God, or questioned His goodness?

CHAPTER 4

On a Treasure Hunt

After three years at the temp agency I took a job back at ORU as assistant alumni director. Working on campus meant meeting many students who would drop by my office to talk about their desires for marriage, career aspirations, and dreams. I understood their longings better now, through my own experiences.

One spring the campus chaplain asked if I would be part of a women's conference, presenting a workshop on "Finding Joy in Singleness."

"Ugh" was my first reaction. Why a workshop on *this* topic? My interest in being a speaker had been growing, so the invitation was appealing. But why did it have to be on *singleness*?

Irrational fear filled my soul, thinking that speaking on "singleness" might somehow mean getting locked into this season, becoming known as someone single, and being single long enough to have something to say about it!

How awful and unthinkable!! How did I ever end up here when

since 13 years old what I wanted most was to be married?!

"Oh well," I finally concluded. "Surely there is something to say in this one workshop." So I prepared with diligence, sharing about the principles of having a vision and being willing to wait. I told about the dream of the Road with the Roses. They loved that vision. It seemed to strike faith in their hearts for similar dreams.

One successful workshop led to subsequent invitations over the next several years, often on this topic of singleness. Several students shared my stories with their pastors, so invitations came to speak for singles retreats across the country.

Though not crazy about the topic, each time would lead to a new revelation or truth about how God works amidst our sufferings. It felt like finding a hidden treasure in the murky, dark depths of the sea.

A timeless principle became personally true -- if we can take our own sufferings and turn them into stories of inspiration for others, there is a redemption of sorts, a sense that, at least in part, our sufferings are not in vain.

> If we can take our own sufferings and turn them into stories of inspiration for others, there is a redemption of sorts, a sense that, at least in part, our sufferings are not in vain.

Years went on. Toni kept having more babies, boy after boy after boy (at the time of this writing she has seven boys and three girls, yes TEN children!). Each time that she called to announce the good news of her pregnancy, internal voices were shouting, "You are falling SO far behind!"

Other friends were having children too, and a knack for entertaining meant I hosted the showers and parties, on my wedding china, celebrating my dreams fulfilled in the lives of others.

One night was uniquely memorable. While back in the bedroom getting ready for bed, my roommate, Kim, and her fiancé, Greg, were listening to music in the living room, choosing songs for their approaching wedding.

A favorite song was playing on the stereo, the exact one I had secretly dreamed of having for my wedding. My heart sank realizing Kim was selecting that exact song. The hot tears rolled as, once again, not only was I losing a roommate, but also one more unique thing for my wedding day.

"I have got to quit talking to everyone," I reasoned. "Otherwise, by the time I get married, all the great ideas will have been taken."

In that moment, amidst thoughts of fear and loss, I heard the gentle voice of the Lord say,

Lynette, I'm the God of the Universe, the God of all creativity. I have dreams and ideas no one has even thought of yet. If you will lavishly invest and sow into your friends' lives, celebrating their joy, investing yourself in their dreams, when your time comes you will not be short-changed. Instead, you will be fuller, richer, more alive with ideas and creativity than you can imagine. Do not hold back. Enter in; enjoy; celebrate with your friends.

His voice of Truth came like a warm, comforting blanket there in that dark room. Feelings of being left out were replaced with a sense of privilege, of getting to share in the joy of friends.

There in the bedroom that night, I decided to be an *investor*. When the celebrations of others only accentuated unfulfilled dreams, I would invest and enter into their joy. Instead of running and hiding, languishing in agony and pain, I would instead pour out on their behalf the ideas, dreams, and visions I wanted to save for my own gain.

Years later in his popular book, *The Purpose-Driven Life*, Rick Warren would open his first chapter with essentially the same truth: "It's not about you." Making our lives about a bigger purpose, focusing on others, and serving and investing, are indeed the keys to lasting fulfillment.

It is ironic, is it not? Giving away in order to gain. Sowing out that we might reap. Pouring forth in order to have our own cups filled.

The story of the small boy who gave his two fish and five loaves to Jesus is one that both challenges and encourages. His small lunch, when put in the Hands of the Master, fed more than 5,000, with basketfuls left over.

> What we have to offer may seem insignificant; we may even give it begrudgingly. Still, in God's Almighty Hands, what we give gets multiplied.

What we have to offer may seem insignificant; we may even give it begrudgingly. Still, in God's Almighty Hands, what we give gets multiplied. As my friend, speaker/author Bob Harrison often says, "The smallest your seed will ever be is when it is in your own hand."

It was a bold step of faith to make such a decision that night in my room. Little did I know how often I would recommit to it, over and over, in the years to come.

CONSIDER THESE QUESTIONS

Have you ever felt jealous of friends who were living your dreams relative to relationships?

Describe an experience when you found your own story has brought hope and help to others.

What might you have to offer in the spirit of being an "investor?"

CHAPTER 5

Set Apart but Not Aside

Professionally, my twenties and thirties held rewarding times of growth, yet even on the job front I often fought discouragement. While friends were getting raises, buying homes, and putting money in 401(k) programs, I was plugging away on one small salary, waiting for a promotion and a raise.

What about so many dreams and aspirations, not to mention the man on the longer-than-expected road with the roses? Faced with insignificant roles at work and few staff or mentors to look to, things felt more like a mishmash than a well-planned, God-led process.

On one business trip Mom accompanied me to do an alumni meeting in New York City. We enjoyed the excitement of Manhattan in between meetings.

Lying in our twin beds one night, talking about the city and the needs so obvious among those millions of people, we both began to weep, sensing the Lord's heart for New York.

As we prayed together, somewhere in a small corner of my heart the small seed of a dream started growing – the dream of one day living in New York City, regardless of how unlikely and unrealistic it seemed.

Turning 30 prompted the decision to go back and see the counselor from ORU. I was discouraged about the job situation. Friends were nearly all married now, having children, leading lives of my dreams, while I was still waiting.

Once again the counselor helped sort the real issues. This time it was not about personal brokenness but rather the sense of powerlessness -- feeling like there were no real choices while the things I desired most were being refused or delayed on every side.

Together, he and I laid out several ways to feel more empowered. After just a few sessions there was new hope and motivation to keep walking and taking a few new steps, professionally and personally.

> The call to be an investor was again the challenge; right there in the waiting, smack dab in the middle of the desert.

The call to be an investor was again the challenge; right there in the waiting, smack dab in the middle of the desert. I had to discover new skills for coping, then plow ahead with what was in hand.

Like the dream of moving to New York, the dream for marriage was ever present. Most of the time things felt fine, but holidays were especially hard. Everyone seemed to have someone on New Year's Eve, or a date for Christmas parties.

In 1998, while writing my annual Christmas letter, it struck me that the "We Won't Wait Past '88" phrase would rhyme again, 10 years later. Who would have ever thought this wait would continue all these years?

At times when waves of despair would threaten, the Lord brought needed encouragement in creative ways.

One such evening I was manning a table at an alumni event in Tulsa. A guy I had been interested in and dated for a while was there with another woman. I felt rejected and alone. Discouraging thoughts flooded: *Surely my meager talks to insignificant groups over the years have meant nothing of real value. Maybe my life is just a big joke anyway. I talk to others about having hope, faith, and vision, yet here I am with none of my own.*

Right then a young woman I did not know came hurriedly over to the table. "You're Lynette Troyer, aren't you?" she asked. "Yes," I said. "You probably don't remember me but I heard you speak at ORU about five years ago," she continued. "What you said made a huge impact on my life and I decided to wait as long as it would take to find God's best. Today is my thirtieth birthday and because of your example, I'm still waiting. So if you ever wondered if your life counts for anything, I am here to tell you it does! Like you, I am waiting as long as it takes for God to bring His best!"

Needless to say, I wanted to weep and weep, not for sorrow, but out of gratitude. The Lord had sent this woman right at that moment, in the midst of deep despair, to tell me to keep holding on, that it was worth it, that the Road with the Roses was not just about me, but about all the other fellow sojourners walking the same road.

What a powerful, precious word. Like discovering manna in the desert, I was fed. More importantly, others had also been fed through the years. That morsel of hope provided courage to go on.

There was another similar moment…

I had been to church one Sunday morning and sat toward the back of the auditorium, a seat that provided a view across most of the audience.

It seemed like the church was filled with mostly couples that day, each one sitting there cozy and together. One woman was giving her husband a neck rub. Another man was stroking his girlfriend's hair. It appeared that everyone was happily paired, while I sat there alone.

I recognized many I had counseled in my ORU office, encouraging them to have hope when, at their young age of 20, they wondered if their dream would ever come true. Now they sat there with their marriage dreams fulfilled, while I, 10 years their senior, still waited.

The drive home felt sad and hopeless, a familiar feeling, like being left out and forgotten. Pondering the Lord's seeming inattention to my dreams, His familiar voice whispered softly,

"I have set you apart, but not aside."

Wow. This resonated like a strong, invigorating wind. If it were so, that I was set apart and not aside, then it was a position of preference and honor, an esteemed place that God had for some reason chosen, and in a sense, entrusted to me.

> Each of us is set apart in some area of life -- chosen, appointed, preferred rather than forgotten.

Each of us is set apart in some area of life -- chosen, appointed, preferred rather than forgotten. The enemy of our souls will tell us otherwise, that we are cast off and set aside. When others receive answers to prayers, it is so tempting to doubt and question rather than believe God's timing will prove no less perfect for us.

I love gardening for many reasons, not the least of which is seeing firsthand how every vegetable and flower must be planted at a certain time. Each requires unique tending and comes to fruitfulness and full beauty at varying seasons. In the same way, we are all uniquely planted and can trust in God's timing to make every detail of our lives fruitful and beautiful.

One gift of growing older is having more and more examples to illustrate this truth. Time and again we realize that all along God is attentive, active, engaged on our behalf, even when in our limited scope it appears otherwise.

If it is true, then, that we are set apart and not aside, then we decide to believe, no matter what it looks like. Hope *is* a choice, not a feeling.

CONSIDER THESE QUESTIONS

Do you ever feel "powerless" in important areas of your life such as work or relationships? How can you be more empowered?

What "dream seeds" are growing in your heart right now relative to dreams beyond relationships?

CHAPTER 6

Blind Date Queen

After 10 years of working at ORU, I accepted a new job with global accounting and consulting firm, Deloitte & Touche. The first six months were exciting but stressful in new ways. Oftentimes I questioned the decision to make a move. Had I missed it? Was I just trying in human hands to bring about excitement and miraculous change? And underneath it all was the ever-present desire just to be married and have a family.

"If my husband had come along by now I would not be facing these decisions anyway," I reasoned. Thirty-five and still alone, the Road with the Roses seemed like an old, faded memory in many ways. Maybe it was just a nice notion, a fantasy of sorts, a mechanism to parlay the pain. Whatever it was, it simply had not happened.

About this time, my sister, Brenda, got married at age 33. I honestly enjoyed all the festivities leading up to her wedding. Brenda, "Bean" as I affectionately call her, certainly deserved this dream come true. It was she and I who had fasted and prayed together every Monday during lunch for three years. We would meet at her apartment and petition the Lord to bring us our husbands and the families we desired.

I was encouraged that His answer for her meant He had heard our prayers and that perhaps mine, too, would not be forgotten. We gladly welcomed Jean Eric Hendryx into our lives; my new brother.

Meanwhile, speaking opportunities were growing. Though many things about my career were enjoyable, speaking had become a first and favorite love. It was in those times, whether speaking to a crowd or just a few eager hearts around my kitchen table, that I felt the greatest sense of purpose and destiny.

On the relationship front, it had been years since my last serious relationship. By this time I could have been called "the blind date queen." Not a title I wanted, but one you gain when you are single for a long time and everyone knows you want to be married.

> By this time I could have been called "the blind date queen." Not a title I wanted, but one you gain when you are single for a long time and everyone knows you want to be married.

In a moment of exasperation one day, I pondered how many blind dates I must have been on. "Hmmm...roughly X number per year, for X number of years, equals...65. Yes, 65 blind dates!" No wonder I felt worn out by this unsuccessful dating technique!

A dear friend, Barbara, was now calling about yet one more—a friend of a friend—and, "He's handsome, single, and an orthopedic surgeon," she exclaimed.

"He does sound intriguing," I surmised. He called for a first date. The attraction was immediate, and within two short weeks we were talking every day. I was more flipped over this man than any before. He loved the Lord and had all the credentials. He would make the wait so worth every tear and every pain!

The next three months were joyful, until he began expressing hesitation (no surprise). "I'm just not sure I have the feelings I need to have," he would say. I responded with, "Feelings follow commitment, and maybe if you were more committed you would have feelings." (Too bad I hadn't seen the movie *He's Just Not That Into You*. Seriously, it could have helped!)

We were walking along the bridge at Tulsa River Parks one night when he dropped the inevitable bomb. "There isn't a future in this, Lynette," he tried to say gently. "I've been praying and asking the Lord to give me the feelings, but they aren't coming. I wanted you to know so I wouldn't lead you on and hurt your heart."

Hurt my heart? I wanted to scream, "You just threw it over the bridge, thank you very much. What is your problem? What is every man in the universe's problem?" I drove away from his house and over to my parents', sobbing again with tears too familiar.

> What is your problem? What is every man in the universe's problem?

While the relationship technically ended, I kept hoping we could work things out. We decided to have a friendship, which did little more than keep my hope alive for four more years. Yes, four more agonizing years of hoping and praying things would change.

God used the experience to teach me many beneficial things about sacrifice, patience, and faith. Still, I honestly do not know how I hung on so long except that I loved him deeply and felt God was in it.

In calling it "friendship" he could dive in deeper without feeling responsible for my heart. I, on the other hand, was in far too deep emotionally to try and just be friends. A configuration like this rarely, if ever, works, but I was determined to give it every chance to succeed.

Finally, four years after the "friendship" started, I called it off completely. It was one of the most heartwrenching, agonizing, and important things I ever had to do -- walk away, at the age of 37, having invested so much for so long, without any sign or hope of anyone else on the horizon. For my own sanity and ability to pursue broader dreams, there was no other choice but to completely let go.

Over dinner at one of our favorite restaurants, I laid it out for him and said with strong conviction, "It's over. I need to move on and be free from the hope that is consistently deferred when investing in you and our relationship. The friendship definition doesn't work for me; I want more. The only relationship worth pursuing is one that both people are mutually committed to and working toward marriage. You have been clear. Now I have to be the same."

I drove home that night knowing it was the right thing to do, yet fighting off a deeper-than-ever sense of raw, utter hopelessness.

CONSIDER THESE QUESTIONS

What do you believe distinguishes "friendship" between guys and girls in contrast to being "romantically involved?"

What "arrangement" are you really after right now in relationships?

How can you communicate these expectations?

At what point in a relationship is it right to communicate your expectations regarding the future of the relationship?

CHAPTER 7

New York, New York

Amidst the heartbreak of the relationship ending, I kept pouring energy and efforts into the marketing role at Deloitte in Tulsa, while still dreaming about a move to New York City.

A transfer offer eventually came and, amidst fond farewells after 19 years in Oklahoma, all my earthly possessions were piled on the moving truck. Off to the Big Apple I went!

From the first day, New York City has been one of the most exciting adventures of my life. Except for family and friends in other cities, every favorite thing is within reach in Manhattan -- amazing food and restaurants, the best shopping in the world, the finest in arts and entertainment.

The move brought refreshment to my soul and an increase in faith, watching this one huge life dream coming to pass.

A first goal was finding a good church, which I did, plus a wonderful home fellowship group, reminiscent of Tulsa days. How fun to be in a city where roughly 60 percent of the residents are single.

Running in Central Park was joyful, and walking the streets I marveled at the path leading to New York. There had indeed been a strategy, a plan in motion, yet one not fully visible much of the time.

> When one dream is on hold, go live others.

I still hoped for the man on the Road with the Roses, but in the meantime, this new adventure was fulfilling and invigorating. A life lesson was also taking shape – when one dream is on hold, go live others.

A year later, in August, an offer too good to refuse came my way -- the position of vice president at a major NYC public relations firm. I left Deloitte on positive terms to embrace yet another professional adventure.

The new job was crazy, stressful, yet adding to the résumé. One new colleague quickly became a close friend. We went to lunch often and talked openly about our lives.

The first day we met I had noticed on his desk a picture of he and another man, their arms around one another. Turns out it was his partner, the person who had prompted his move from San Francisco to New York City the year before.

I started praying for this dear new friend, and in doing so, God would reveal pictures in my mind of what He (God) desired to do in his life.

Near Christmas, my friend asked for prayer since he was going in for plastic surgery to remove deep acne scars from his face. I said that, yes, I would pray for him, and added that, in fact, "I've already been praying." I shared my sense that God loved him deeply and wanted to hold a stronger place in his life.

At this point my friend, so moved by the care and concern, put his face in his hands and began to weep. He told me through tears that it was this kind of touch from God he was wanting, how all his life he had felt ugly and unworthy. "My scars run much deeper than my face," he said.

I took his hand and prayed for his surgery, asking God to touch his life in a powerful, personal way. A short time later he and his partner flew to Miami to be married. When they returned, I invited the two of them, along with another guy from work, over for dinner, elegantly served on my wedding china.

Spending several hours planning the menu and preparing the four-course meal, I was struck by how different things were than I would have expected. By now I envisioned hosting families in my home, husband and children by my side. Instead, here I was hosting three gay friends, pulling out all the stops to celebrate them and extend love. My sweet mom said to me that afternoon, "Enjoy tonight honey, but be careful," to which I laughed and responded, "Mom, if ever there was a night your daughter is safe with three men in her home, it's tonight!"

It was a marvelous evening with great food and conversation. After washing all the wedding china by hand, I crawled into bed thanking God for the surprise gifts in life – different than the gifts we might choose, but nonetheless rich and sweet.

Have you ever been given one of those gifts you just know is a "re-gift," or something you would *never* buy? Later, after giving it a whirl, you discover how much you like it, and you might even call it a treasure.

This season in my life was revealing this exact principle. Staying open to surprise packages often leads to surprise joys.

> Staying open to surprise packages often leads to surprise joys.

The economic downturn in New York was taking a big toll on many companies at the time, including mine. I got laid off from the PR firm and fortunately took a job back at Deloitte, working for a former boss who was now in a new role.

Returning to Deloitte and new responsibilities, I was longing for more meaning and fulfillment, so I began to focus on what my core life message might be.

Over several months I kept coming back to the concept of *purpose*—defining it, living by it waiting on purpose, dating on purpose, and so forth. Everything I had experienced and all I stood for seemed to connect to this theme of purpose.

Evenings and weekends, I worked on taking my speaking career to the next level, hiring a friend to design a website, and another one to come up with a logo and "look" for the Lynette Troyer brand. Devoting time to these dreams brought new energy to my current job.

That summer some dear friends and I rented a house in the Hamptons, on Long Island, a welcome city getaway. Little did we know that in just a few short weeks, the World Trade Center towers would fall and tragedy would strike our beloved New York City.

The day of 9/11 I left my apartment early to take a car service up to our Deloitte office in Hartford, Connecticut. It was the office farthest away from Manhattan and I almost did not go due to a bad case of laryngitis.

But go I did, and at 8:45 that morning our team in the office, along with the rest of the world, sat stunned and heartbroken as the tragedy began to unfold.

Had I not been in Hartford that day I would have likely been in the middle of the chaos. It was just the time I typically passed through the World Trade Center concourse heading to the office at the World Financial Center or in Jersey City.

Many colleagues watched as people threw themselves from burning buildings. By God's sovereign plan I was not in those buildings that day. It took months to fully recover emotionally, and my sense of loss was nothing compared to so many thousands of others. I am forever marked by that day.

CONSIDER THESE QUESTIONS

Have you ever been involved in a church, and would you be drawn to a small group of people committed to "doing life together"?

What "surprise packages" have you discovered in your life, bringing unexpected gifts that you now treasure?

What one dream might you really want to pursue right now? What ways can you proactively go for it starting this week?

CHAPTER 8

Saying "Yes" in the Desert

Friends and I bonded together to move on with life. Pursuing a variety of passions helped. Preparing to speak for a major leadership event, I was thinking about the need to have some resources for sale at the conference. Where do I even start? I had nothing more than a nice new logo and a basic website. What did I, Lynette Troyer, have to write about or say?

One month later, with my entire family in Maui, I spoke to a crowd of 400 business leaders. I talked about "7 Principles of Purpose" and explained how the leaders in attendance could build purpose-driven teams.

It was amazing to realize that during years of insignificance, while longing for mentors and having none, reading books as my only training, experimenting with a small staff of students and volunteers, God was equipping me with tools and concepts I could now offer to others.

Seldom do we recognize the crucial, if not essential, preparation He is orchestrating in the desert seasons of our lives. It is often in these seasons, when things feel dry and desolate, that we can choose to grow deeper, becoming truly mature.

> Seldom do we recognize the crucial, if not essential, preparation He is orchestrating in the desert seasons of our lives.

A favorite excerpt from C.S. Lewis' book "The Screwtape Letters" speaks to this when Satan talks to his apprentice Wormwood, about "the Enemy" (God) and what pleases Him. He says,

Sooner or later He withdraws, if not in fact, at least from their conscious experience, all those supports and incentives. He leaves the creature to stand up on its own legs - to carry out from the will alone duties which have lost all relish. It is during such trough periods, much more than during the peak periods, that it is growing into the sort of creature He wants it to be. Hence the prayers offered in the state of dryness are those which please Him best...He wants them to learn to walk and must therefore take away His hand; and if only the will to walk is really there He is pleased even with their stumbles. Do not be deceived, Wormwood. Our cause is never more in danger, than when a human, no longer desiring, but intending, to do our Enemy's will, looks round upon a universe from which every trace of Him seems to have vanished, and asks why he has been forsaken, and still obeys.[4]

What powerful truth. Like Joseph in the prison, Jesus in the Garden of Gethsemane, Paul in prison, Esther as an orphan queen putting her life on the line, each of us will at some point have the opportunity to say "Yes, I am willing to endure the suffering," and still choose to believe.

The next day in Hawaii was my fortieth birthday. Celebrating with family was a gift, but I awoke that morning with a heavy heart. The excitement of the previous day still lingered, but the realization

I was now 40, still unmarried with no children, was bearing down hard.

Sitting in a small café for breakfast with Bean and Jean, I could not keep the hot tears from flowing. I should have been so excited about the success of the previous day and how God was opening up many exciting new doors. Truthfully, I was excited. But still, the deep desire for a husband and children had not gone away. Being honest with the longing while still enjoying the gifts He was giving was a tough tension to manage.

I have found this tension between joy and sorrow to be a common experience of the human heart. It is a fine balance between living honestly yet not giving way to despair.

Many go to one extreme or the other. On one end there is denial: "Who needs men? I'm fine on my own." On the other end, desperation: "Do you know someone, anyone, who might be the one for me?"

Neither end of the spectrum was appealing, so I chose to find some sort of middle ground: "Yes I do want to be married, no I don't understand why it has not happened, and yes in the meantime I'm living other dreams."

Returning from Hawaii and throughout that year, I refined my message while exploring further ways to expand the speaking career. Meanwhile, work at Deloitte was flourishing, and I was grateful for a solid job that paid the bills.

⁴ C. S. Lewis, *The Screwtape Letters* (New York: Macmillon Publishing Co. Inc., 1977), 39.

CONSIDER THESE QUESTIONS

Have you felt a call to "go deeper" lately?

What about the tension between joy and sorrow – how do you practically manage this and live honestly on both ends of the spectrum?

CHAPTER 9

Life Is About to Change

The Christmas before turning 40, I was home for the holidays. Mom and I were enjoying a favorite pastime – sitting in the family room looking at magazines.

Looking through one called *Charisma*, Mom came upon a full-page ad promoting a new church that had started in Times Square right after 9/11.

"Miracle on 44th Street" the ad read in the headline, describing a group of visionary leaders who had come to Manhattan to begin this new church in a historic theatre on 44th Street, just off Times Square.

Four photos on the ad showed the men leading the congregation. "These guys look like ORU guys," Mom said. "Have you heard of this church?" I had not, and the first Sunday back after the holidays I visited Morning Star New York.

Every aspect of the service was excellent, the worship music the best I had enjoyed in awhile. The message by Ron Lewis (one of the men on the ad) was inspiring. I was especially impressed when he came over after the service, extended his hand, and welcomed me. In many churches it is rare to ever see the pastor anywhere other than the podium.

Over the next few months I attended regularly and got increasingly involved. I met the other leaders and made new friends. Morning Star was part of an international family of churches all over the world (EveryNation.org), which drew an eclectic, multi-ethnic congregation.

For the weeks to come, Ron, along with Pastor Rice Broocks and NFL player-turned-pastor Tim Johnson, ministered in their home congregations in Raleigh and Nashville on Sunday mornings, then flew up to do our services in New York on Sunday nights. They kept this hectic schedule for over a year.

Along with being my pastors, Ron, Rice, and Tim became my friends. Realizing my love for speaking, they started opening doors with other Every Nation events and churches. It was a year of exciting growth for the church.

Over the previous year and a half I had been casually pursuing an off-and-on relationship with a friend from Canada. He was a strong Christian, interesting, achieved, a few years older than I was, and never married. On his occasional visits to New York we would go to dinner or for a run in the park, at times emailing in between.

> At my age I wondered if chemistry was overrated. Perhaps it could evolve as we pursued something more?

In many ways he had the qualities I envisioned, but somehow there was just never the spark or chemistry. At my age I wondered if chemistry was overrated. Perhaps it could evolve as we pursued something more?

Our friendship went through various phases, but he had recently concluded it was just not "there" for him. In my heart I agreed.

One night drifting off to sleep, thinking of our relationship, I whispered to myself and the Lord, "I just want someone who I am so excited about I cannot fall asleep!" Little did I know how many sleepless nights were just around the corner.

CONSIDER THESE QUESTIONS

What aspects of this part of Lynette's story do you find most inspiring, challenging, or perhaps even frustrating?

CHAPTER 10

Faith Becomes Sight

I will never forget when the "aha moment" that would change my life forever occurred. It was a Sunday evening and I had walked over to chat with Ron after he had given the evening message.

He was the full-time pastor by now, but we still knew each other only from a distance. His transparent style when he preached had allowed everyone to see his heart and the passion with which he loved God and people.

As he and I sat there this particular night, chatting on the front row amidst the post-service crowd, out of the blue it was as if a rushing, powerful revelation brought together every hope and aspiration I had ever had about a husband. There in living color, it all came together in Ron.

My mouth kept talking but my mind was overwhelmed. "Oh no, this couldn't be," I reasoned. "He is divorced with four boys; this is not the vision I have had. But he is so amazing and seems like everything I have dreamed. Oh, but I can't imagine these circumstances. A minister instead of a corporate guy?"

Thoughts were racing while I tried to act cool and calm. We finished a friendly but professional conversation in which he shared more in depth about the circumstances that had led him to our church in New York. It was the first time we had talked on any sort of personal level.

Leaving the service, a myriad of thoughts were spinning through my head. In the taxi all the way home and then climbing into bed, all I could think about was how incredible he was. Achieved, funny, handsome, and winsome, I suspected he was close to my age.

Could this really be, God? The excitement and thought of it was more than I could contain. I barely slept an hour the entire night.

For the next number of weeks I pondered and prayed through the possibilities, sharing them with Toni, my parents, and Bean. Their encouragement was to be open to the idea even though the circumstances were different than envisioned.

> I knew all too well the pattern of liking someone from a distance, being hopefully certain he was my future husband, then crushed when he was not.

Hope and desire grew but I continued to guard my heart and emotions, determined not to bring the possibility up with anyone at church, and certainly not with Rice or Ron. I knew all too well the pattern of liking someone from a distance, being hopefully certain he was my future husband, then crushed when he was not. I also knew the "manipulate circumstances to get noticed" routine.

This time would be different; I would wait for his expression of commitment before letting my heart go. Still, night after night, I barely slept a wink.

Weeks progressed and we continued talking casually after church, always in the company of others. In my newfound revelation I sensed he might be coming to a similar openness.

A few months from the first epiphany moment, I was heading to an Every Nation conference as a workshop speaker. Ron was also attending and we ran into each other in the lobby. He and the conference host asked who was introducing me, and since no one had been designated, Ron offered to do it.

I thought to myself, "OK, this is going to be interesting. For the first time he will get a firsthand look at the passion and strength that are a core part of who I am, especially when speaking."

The room was crowded, the first of two workshops went well, and the attendees responded with enthusiasm. I thought it comical when one man came up afterward and evidently thought Ron was a close friend of mine. I overheard him saying, "She is an amazing speaker, a national treasure, no maybe an international treasure" (you would have thought I paid the guy!), to which Ron responded with a warm laugh, "Well, yes she is!"

In between workshops Ron and I sat for a few minutes and chatted. I began getting nervous thinking he might be overwhelmed by what he saw. *"As a speaker/pastor himself, he may prefer a quiet, low-key woman,"* I wondered. Funny how many negative assumptions rise up when you feel vulnerable.

Nervous about his perceptions and eager to appear approachable and nonthreatening, I mentioned, "I'll be off work on Monday and if you want to grab coffee, maybe we could work it out."

A week or two earlier at church, Ron had casually mentioned the idea of meeting for coffee sometime in the neighborhood. His apartment was not too far from mine, so it was just a random idea in the course of friendly conversation.

The next day back in New York for the Sunday service, I regretted ever mentioning the coffee idea. Maybe I had been too presumptuous and, after all, I was still waiting for him to take the initiative to pursue something more.

The following day about 10 AM the phone rang. It was Ron! He had an open slot in his schedule, and would I want to meet for that coffee? "Sure," I said. We agreed on one o'clock.

I was full of anticipation. This would be the first time we had ever been alone. I expected it to be a real indicator of whether there was an attraction for more than just friendship, and what the level of connection outside group settings might be.

He rang the doorbell and came upstairs. I asked if he would mind sitting for a few minutes while I put a last coat of polish on my nails. (Ron said later he liked how "relaxed and real" that seemed.) The conversation was easy. He looked so handsome in his camel-colored v-neck and jeans.

> I was full of anticipation. This would be the first time we had ever been alone.

We walked a few blocks to Columbus Bakery and ordered our coffees, then sat at an outside table and talked for a good while.

He shared about his divorce, acknowledging his own failings. I was impressed with how "whole" he seemed. He spoke lovingly about his four sons and his unwavering commitment to them.

I asked questions and spoke about my own journey some. The conversation was easy, fun, and natural. I was being drawn to this man and was excited to sense the same from him.

Weeks went by and we continued speaking occasionally at church. I hosted a small dinner party one evening in my apartment to introduce the church leadership team to some of my more established New York friends.

I purposefully planned it for a Monday so Ron could be included. He was typically flying into the city on Sunday afternoons, then back to Raleigh on Tuesday evenings to be with his boys the rest of each week.

It was a fun dinner party, and I found out later that on the way home Ron was riding with our friends Dave and Chris, the associate pastors whom I had grown to know quite well.

Ron said to them, "Lynette seems like an incredible woman. Does she want to be married?" Chris told him indeed I did, to which Ron said, "She is attractive, successful, and a terrific cook. Why would she still be single?" Chris explained I had a list of qualities I was waiting for and evidently had not found anyone yet who fit the list.

The next day Ron called Dave to discuss some church business, and ended by saying, "Can you ask Chris if there is any reason I would not qualify for Lynette's list?" Dave told Ron later, "Chris thinks it may be a fit!"

Ron left a very kind voice mail on my machine later that day. "Lynette, this is Pastor Ron and I just wanted to thank you for dinner last night. It was great and you were so kind to host us. Oh, and sorry I left before cleaning up or vacuuming your floor!"

A big smile crossed my face, but I wondered why he referred to himself as "Pastor Ron." Maybe he was just doing the nice, southern thing and was not really interested in anything beyond friendship.

A couple days later he called again and we had a wonderful conversation. It was easy and natural in a way not experienced in so long.

Hope was growing and the staunch guard around my heart was softening. Still, the intention to wait on both God and Ron was clear. If—*IF*—this was my time, then I knew I could, in many ways, sit back and watch it unfold.

CONSIDER THESE QUESTIONS

What aspects of this part of Lynette's story do you find most inspiring, challenging, or perhaps even frustrating?

I Think I Love You

A few more weeks passed, and by now I was certain Ron had some level of interest, though no overt indications had yet been made between us. We had a few more casual phone conversations, often about church-related things.

One Sunday I offered to help him purchase a new carpet for the apartment he was renting on the Upper West Side. We enjoyed a casual shopping experience and as we were finishing up he said, "You've been such a help and encouragement, Lynette. Can I take you to dinner to show my sincere appreciation?"

"I'd love that," I responded, hoping in my heart this would be the time to discuss our growing attraction.

Ron came by in a taxi and we headed over to a lovely restaurant new to both of us, called Town. It was elegant and the food was delicious.

We were just beginning the main course when he initiated the conversation I had been waiting more than forty years to hear. "I really appreciate this chance to have dinner," he began. "As you know, I'm a pastor, and I want to assure you it's not my regular practice to take out women in the church," he smiled nervously. "I'd like to be up front with you about something and possibly get a little feedback." Inside I was smiling *big*, sensing the direction this conversation was going.

"I think you are an incredible woman," he continued. "I have enjoyed getting to know you and so appreciate the calling on your life. I would be interested in pursuing something more between us, but at the same time want you to know if you are not interested that is fine. I will continue advocating for you, opening up doors whenever I can, and believing in your vision."

At this point he paused, and it was clearly my turn to respond. Such a flood of emotion and excitement were rushing through my heart and mind.

> Now it was happening. An incredible, strong, visionary man was man enough to lay it all out on the table and clearly state his intentions.

These were the words I had been waiting to hear for years. Now it was happening. An incredible, strong, visionary man was man enough to lay it all out on the table and clearly state his intentions.

On the one hand I wanted to blurt out, "Yes, yes, yes, let's go for it, I'm interested!" But what I did was pause to relish the moment. I wanted it to linger so I could enjoy a few brief moments deciding how to respond to such an amazing statement of intention.

Finally, after what seemed like an eternity but was really about 10 seconds, I calmly responded. "I appreciate you bringing this up and have actually been thinking and praying about it for some time—another long pause—and I want to go for it!" I was smiling from ear to ear.

Ron breathed a visible sigh of relief and responded, "Oh, this is great." Suddenly, it was as if everyone in the room disappeared and the two of us were sitting there alone, staring at our future.

I honestly do not remember the next few sentences, but I do remember asking after a bit more chatting, "So what do we do next?"

I loved Ron's answer. "As soon as possible I want to meet with Rice and his wife Jody. Rice has been my pastor for 20 years and I want this relationship to be transparent from the beginning."

We talked more over the delectable desserts, then hopped in a cab up to our neighborhood. In one way it felt as if we had been friends for years. In another way it felt entirely new and a bit awkward.

I put my hand on his knee during the ride home and he gave me a sweet hug as we said good-bye that unforgettable evening.

It was surreal as I called Mom, Bean, and Toni, saying amidst my overwhelming yet secure sense of excitement, "Tonight my entire life changed."

In the coming weeks I would discover even more clearly how true that was, and how exciting this new season was about to become.

CONSIDER THESE QUESTIONS

What aspects of this part of Lynette's story do you find most inspiring, challenging, or perhaps even frustrating?

CHAPTER 12

Start Spreading the News

S oon after we flew to Nashville to spend a day with Rice and Jody. We sat for hours around their dining room table, sharing lots of stories, talking about Ron's journey and mine. I asked any and every question I had, wanting full assurance that his divorce was biblically permitted and that pursuing a relationship was in the will of God for both of our lives.

Rice and others had walked with Ron for years, through every trial and testing. They had watched his responses to life's challenges and were now rejoicing at what seemed to be God's beginning of restoration for him.

Their wisdom and perspectives, coupled with the counsel from my parents and closest friends, brought necessary confirmation. A decision involving marriage should never be made in a vacuum. Our closest friends and trusted advisors were giving a resounding "yes," and so were we.

At this point our top priority was caring for the hearts of his sons.

If we handled this right, our chances for their acceptance of me would be high. On the other hand, rushing into things or letting our own desires dictate could result in years of mistrust and resistance on their part.

> A decision involving marriage should never be made in a vacuum.

Ron was sensitive to the timing and had a conversation with each of them individually. The time to bring everyone else in on the news finally came.

I was hosting our annual PureLife women's conference in New York with hundreds of women from many cities in attendance. Friday night I opened with a talk about "Waiting on Purpose," sharing my twenty-plus year journey of waiting on God to bring my husband, talking about the challenges we all face in seasons of waiting. The audience and I shared moments of laughter and tears. I told about the Road with the Roses. I did not, however, divulge news about Ron and our relationship.

Sunday evening was the closing session, when the conference attendees joined our congregation for the final service together. Ron was speaking that night and had decided to talk about "The God of All Restoration." It would be the first time he shared details about his personal journey through divorce and other sufferings.

His message was powerful. He talked about how years before, in a one-year period, his mom and dad were both in and out of the hospital numerous times. His wife of many years wanted out of the marriage and the ministry. He resigned his church in Raleigh to protect it from any backlash of the divorce while his boys were in the greatest turmoil of their lives. As he spoke he drew stories from the Bible that related to the wilderness journey each of us will face at various times in our lives.

Bringing the message to a close, he said, "I am happy to tell you tonight, that in spite of the dark valleys I have been through, because of the faithfulness of God, everything is working out all right for Pastor Ron. My parents are both improved and doing well. My sons are individually finding their way through adversity. I get to lead this great congregation in New York City, and the 'gift of suffering' has provided a unique ability to relate to those who are hurting. Best of all…God has brought someone wonderful into my life."

As he made this last statement you could hear an audible buzz and a few gasps begin to ripple through the crowd. Ron paused and looked down on the front row where I was sitting. Keeping his eyes on me, he started walking across the stage, the expectation building in the audience. As he neared my chair, he said, "And it was a real privilege to hear her story all over again on Friday night."

He stopped in front of my chair, reaching out his hand like a prince extending a hand to a princess. I took it, we embraced, and the crowd was going crazy. Women who did not even know us were crying and hugging one another. It was like the best reality TV episode or a heartrending Oprah show!

Hand in hand we walked up on the stage while the applause and cheering kept getting louder. I spontaneously looked up to Heaven and lifted my hand, pointing to God. I was crying, Ron was crying, it seemed like everyone was crying or cheering.

> For so many years I had worried that when my husband came along it would be so anticlimactic. I could almost hear people saying, "Lynette is finally getting married? Good, send pictures."

Pastor Tim Johnson prayed over us, and as we dismissed the service the excitement refused to wane. A few of us went to dinner afterward, relishing in the joy of that unforgettable evening.

For so many years I had worried that when my husband came along it would be so anticlimactic. I could almost hear people saying, "Lynette is finally getting married? Good, send pictures." I never dreamed how much my generous heavenly Father would amaze me with His goodness in all the details, letting hundreds join in the celebration, far over and above my highest dreams!

CONSIDER THESE QUESTIONS

Would you ever be open to marrying someone with children? What are the unique challenges in such a situation? Are there any other "out-of-the-ordinary" scenarios you would or would not be open to?

How important is it to have counsel and accountability when making a decision to marry someone?

How can you spot "wholeness" in someone you're interested in?

How crucial is it for a potential mate to already be healthy vs. being someone with potential?

Who are your "accountability partners" when you make big life decisions?

CHAPTER 13

Showers of Joy

We set our wedding date and I headed into the whirlwind of planning a New York City wedding.

A few months earlier Ron and I, along with a few others, had been ministering to a man coming off serious drugs. We found out later he was a major events producer who had planned many corporate events and several celebrity weddings.

Soon after announcing our engagement, this new friend, Mark, said to us, "I would love to give you my planning expertise as a wedding gift!" I was thrilled, gave him my budget, and he went to work with his creative genius, calling in favors and putting together what would be the wedding of our dreams.

I was reminded of that night back in the bedroom while Kim and Greg were choosing my song for their wedding, recalling what the Lord had spoken, saying, "I have dreams and ideas no one has ever even thought of." Now I was living that word coming to pass.

Meanwhile, friends were planning parties and showers. A shower in Tulsa and three in New York were full of laughter and memories, reflecting on the long Road with the Roses, wrought with richness and tears.

It was evident at each of these beautiful gatherings that the years I had spent attending baby and wedding showers, entering into my friends' joy while longing for my own, was now yielding a return far surpassing any investment. In fact, the sweetness of the celebrations was enhanced by sufferings endured.

> The years I had spent attending baby and wedding showers, entering into my friends' joy while longing for my own, was now yielding a return far surpassing any investment.

I relished every moment of planning, making use of the wonderful perks of living in New York such as the flower district, stationary and paper shops, incredible wedding fairs, and the elaborate china and crystal stores.

For years I had dreamed of having Italian Cream Cake for the reception, but after searching high and low was unable to find a bakery that could make this cake at an affordable price.

Walking in my neighborhood I noticed in a brownstone window some beautiful wedding cakes. I rushed home and visited the website, discovering that Elisa Strauss of Confetti Cakes could use the client's own recipe. I scheduled an appointment, and with my recipe in her hand, she was hired!

Working with Elisa was so much fun, and months later she appeared on the Food Network on one of their dream wedding shows. This was just one example of special gifts the Lord brought me and how fun planning a wedding in NYC was at every turn.

Mom flew into the city one weekend and we went to every single bridal gown store we could find, from Kleinfeld's in Brooklyn to Vera Wang's studio on the Upper East Side. I tried on every dress I loved, from those costing $10,000 to many far more affordable. The dress had to be incredible, but at the same time I was not going to pay an exorbitant price for something worn for only 10 hours.

We found the perfect gown at a place called RK Bridal in the garment district. It was truly my favorite dress of all and amazingly priced at only $800.

Mark was simultaneously designing so many awesome ideas, most of which he was keeping a surprise because, "It's part of the gift," he would say.

We booked the hotel for the reception, found the most beautiful old cathedral-like church on Park Avenue (at no charge, thanks to Ron's relationship with the rector), and every other detail fell perfectly in place.

Meanwhile, Ron was carefully nurturing the hearts of each of his four sons. I often say, "No one wants a stepparent," and it is a complicated thing for a child when a parent is getting married. We prayed and kept trusting God to help us walk in wisdom to successfully blend our family.

Because Ron and I did not live in the same city except for two days a week in NY, I did not have the luxury of getting to know the boys much at all prior to the wedding. I had several brief interactions, but in our case, most of the relationship-building would occur after the wedding.

Meeting Ron's parents went well. They showed much love and welcomed me into the family. One particular gift from Ron's Mom, Eutha, was a remarkable sign of God's lavish goodness.

From a young age, Eutha had been collecting an exquisite pattern of sterling silver flatware called Corsage. Ornate and intricate, her set had every piece imaginable, including the tiny demitasse spoons, twelve or more of every piece. Soon after we were engaged, Ron mentioned his mom wanted to give us this set as a wedding gift.

What Ron and Eutha did not know was that early in my twenties, I would go to the Tulsa Flea Market virtually every Saturday, always stopping by the booth where the sterling silver was for sale. My eyes always went to a set that was especially ornate. I would look at those pieces and dream of having a set of my own. But at $35 for one teaspoon, I simply could not afford that level of investment, so instead, I would gaze upon the beauty and just dream.

Now here I was, some 20 years later, receiving an entire set, even more beautiful than the pattern I had been admiring for years. I knew this gift was planned by the Lord, one more sign of His "exceedingly, abundantly, beyond my highest dreams" answered prayers.

When I shared this story with Eutha, she marveled to think that God would bring her a daughter-in-law, so late in life, who would treasure her set of sterling as much as she had for more than 50 years.

Each time I use her set with my Grandmother's wedding china, I marvel at how God cares about even the smallest desires of our hearts. He loves to lavish us, more than we can imagine. Not one dream or desire goes unnoticed. Even when we wait for years, He never fails to come through. I have seen this play out over and over again in my life and in the lives of so many others. It makes me want to dream bigger so that later I can watch His faithfulness and praise Him even more!

> Not one dream or desire goes unnoticed. Even when we wait for years, He never fails to come through.

CONSIDER THESE QUESTIONS

Do you have any secret desires relative to your dream engagement, wedding, or honeymoon?

Do you make a regular practice of "dreaming on all cylinders" (beyond just dreaming for relationships) and expressing your desires to God?

CHAPTER 14

Here Comes the Bride

The few short months of planning passed quickly as I counted down the hours until I could live every day with my love.

I kept marveling at Ron. He was so strong, full of character and integrity, balanced and wise. We laughed so much and felt connected on many levels.

Our times of prayer were deep. We shared so many of the same values and perspectives on life. Ron celebrated the commitment I made to retain my virginity until our wedding night. We were committed to purity in our relationship from day one, though the chemistry and attraction were intense.

Not everyone comes into marriage the way I did. Many walk in with physical and emotional regrets. The real love story is God's power to restore, cover, heal, and make whole. (More on that later.)

Thanksgiving weekend, I flew to Raleigh to be with Ron and the boys. It would give us a chance to decorate his house for Christmas, plus spend a bit of time with the guys. We shopped for their wedding suits and worked together on getting the house ready for our return from the honeymoon, just a week before Christmas.

At times things were a bit uncomfortable that weekend, all of us getting to know one another in the context of the upcoming marriage. I tried not to push or be too intense, wanting them to feel the freedom to come toward me as they were led. I could only imagine how strange it seemed to them on so many levels. Who ever expects to attend your own parent's wedding to someone other than your mom or dad?

> The real love story is God's power to restore, cover, heal, and make whole.

Ron and I went to premarital counseling, which was a wonderful gift in helping us not only address potential fault lines in ourselves, but crucial in better understanding unique challenges we would face as a blended family. The counselor has been a go-to advisor for us many times since.

The wedding week arrived! Friends started coming in from around the world. Hundreds who had walked with us through tears, sufferings, and so much of life pulled out the stops to be with us. So much for my unfounded fears that by the time I got married, everyone would be so weary they would say, "Please...just send pictures."

I went on a run Friday morning in Central Park, rounding all those familiar bends in awe. I had traversed them so many times without even a clue or glimmer of hope that the man with the roses was on his way. Our two roads were merging now, and the faithfulness of God had proven true.

Two hours later Central Park was the perfect backdrop for our bridesmaid luncheon at Tavern on the Green. I had arranged for a table in the Crystal Room, one of the most beautiful rooms in all of New York City at Christmastime.

At each of their place settings were the bridesmaid gifts in beautiful silver paper, with large frou frou bows. The girls would be wearing their own black dresses for the wedding, so I was giving them black rabbit-fur stoles and long satin gloves, with a sparkling brooch to match.

I presented Mom with a cross-stitched framed Bible verse, one I had started stitching 10 years before and finished up just that week. It was a theme verse through all the years of waiting, "Blessed is she who has believed that what the Lord has told her will be accomplished. Luke 1:45"

Sitting there with my best friends, Mom, and sister, I was reminded of how the gift of relationships surpasses all other gifts in life. Sharing indescribable joy with these women who had carried me in times of grief, prayed so often over dreams, and stood in faith when it felt impossible to believe was a gift beyond words.

In all of our imaginations we could have never thought it would turn out as amazing as this (or take so long)! We all agreed to "keep drinking it in"—every single moment of the weekend.

> It is the gift of relationships that surpasses all other gifts in life.

Ron, his parents, and the boys arrived in town that afternoon and checked into the New Yorker Hotel. The bridal party headed to the church for a quick rehearsal, then over to Tony's Di Napoli, one of our all-time favorite Italian restaurants, the place most of our church members would go every Sunday night after church.

Tony's was the perfect backdrop for the rehearsal dinner. We ate our fill of penné a la vodka and chicken marsala, enjoying two hours of fellowship, not to mention lots of laughs.

Ron had asked several people to share as the tiramisu and NY cheesecake arrived at each table. Certainly the most memorable was that of our oldest son Nathan, age 20 at the time. "This is a joyful occasion and I want to make a toast. Thank you for coming into our family, Lynette. In many ways you are bringing healing to all of us. We praise God for you!"

We were holding back tears, Nathan's words so poignantly reminding us all that this weekend was about God restoring, fulfilling, and completing, as much as looking ahead.

After dinner some walked and others caught cabs over to Rockefeller Center, where many friends were waiting to say hello. Our plans to carol at the famous Christmas Tree were superseded by the incredibly cold temperatures forcing us back inside.

Ron kissed me good-night and put me in a cab. I pondered the joy and our love all the way home. Getting ready for bed on this my last night of singleness, there in the quietness of my cozy little apartment, I was overcome with excitement, so much so that it was nearly 2 AM before I drifted off to sleep.

CONSIDER THESE QUESTIONS

As you read the final chapters of Lynette's story, what stirs in your own heart relative to the dreams of love and marriage? (i.e. inspiration, jealousy, skepticism about your own hopes, etc.)

CHAPTER 15

Glorious Expectation

My body felt tired but my heart was ready to jump out of bed when the alarm rang at 8 AM. I needed to finish packing and wanted to enjoy a few last moments of being alone with the Lord over coffee.

Sentiments I wrote in my journal that morning captured a few of the many thoughts in my heart.

> *It is 8:30 a.m. on the day I will become Mrs. Ron Lewis! What a glorious day, long-awaited, so worth the wait. How could I have ever known the joy, the awesome ways in which God intended to lavish my life?! It is a sunny, beautiful day, no wind but cold. Glory to God for His indescribable gifts. Thank you Lord, for helping me hold out and remember the roses. Forgive me for ever doubting you. Today bring glory to your name, and let your Presence be thick, tangible and supreme!*

Bags in hand, hair and makeup perfect, I left for the hotel where the bridesmaids were waiting in a specially reserved suite.

We had ordered in sandwiches and invited the aunts, cousins, and my future mother-in-laws to join us. What fun to be so high up in the sky overlooking the Empire State Building and other New York sites on such a beautiful December day. We were drinking it in!

> The Lord was the Author of this entire dream-come-true.

With dresses looking stunning, and makeup perfected, we gathered around for prayer, reminding ourselves that the Lord was the Author of this entire dream-come-true. We had prayed together countless times before. Now we stood together, praising Him for His abundant ways.

Guests were already arriving when the wedding party got to the church. Mark, our amazing wedding planner, had been praying months earlier about what the Lord had in mind for the atmosphere that day. The word he got was "Glorious Expectation," so he had planned some incredible moments that would capture this theme.

"One thing people miss at weddings is the moment before the bride comes down the aisle," Mark explained to me weeks before. "We need to create a buildup as everyone anticipates your entrance. Just as the Bride of Christ is anticipating His return, your wedding, Lynette, exemplifies this sense of glorious expectation." I loved these ideas and could not wait to see Mark's plans come to life.

One thing I knew for sure was that the vision of the Road with the Roses would need to be shared with everyone in attendance. It had been such an anchor all these years, amidst doubts and the turbulence of waiting. So I included it as a beautiful insert on silver paper inside the wedding programs. As people waited for the ceremony to begin, they read those words given some 22 years before.

The aisle had roses attached to the end of every pew, reminiscent of the roses on that road. I would walk down the aisle without a bouquet and Mom would hand it to me when Dad passed my hand into his.

One by one my beautiful bridesmaids entered the back of the church from the side doors. The pipe organ played "Jesu Joy of Man's Desiring", and you could feel the glory of God in that place.

With the bridal party in place, two of our ushers took hold of the white carpet rolled up front, which, unbeknownst to us, was filled with hundreds of pink and white rose petals.

The organ played another glorious song as the carpet stretched down the long aisle; glorious expectation filled the sanctuary.

The doors in the back swung open as I stood there waiting with Dad. The organ broke into the exuberant wedding song from *The Sound of Music,* and we began walking down the long aisle amidst the roses I had been dreaming of most my life.

My amazing Ron handed me the bouquet of lots of roses; let the ceremony begin!

For years I planned to include the famous hymn, "Great is Thy Faithfulness." I had sung it over and over in many lonely seasons, often as a statement of faith, having no idea how prayers would ever be answered.

Now, here we were, surrounded by nearly 500 of our family and friends, declaring it again, faith becoming sight. There was hardly a dry eye in the room as everyone sang.

> In rare moments in life, we get to witness dreams coming true right before our eyes, supernatural interventions in circumstances that bring about answered prayer.

In rare moments in life, we get to witness dreams coming true right before our eyes, supernatural interventions in circumstances that bring about answered prayer. This wedding day was, without a doubt, such a dream. Having so many to celebrate with us made it even more wondrous.

Rice gave a short and meaningful personal message (Ron insisted on "short," having done so many long weddings himself through the years!). I tried to drink it all in, but as every bride knows, it happens so fast and in many ways becomes a blur (which is why you need that wedding video!).

We exchanged vows, rings, and then a kiss, turning to face our guests as Rice announced what was music to our ears. "It is my great privilege to introduce to you now, Mr. and Mrs. Ron Lewis."

Applause and cheers erupted as "The Hallelujah Chorus" rang loud from the organ. We walked down the aisle past roses and beaming faces, in awe of our dream-come-true.

Our car navigated holiday traffic while heading toward the Millenium Broadway Hotel across from the historic Lamb's Theatre, the theatre where our church had been meeting since its beginning.

This classic hotel had the old world Hollywood glamour I wanted, made even more beautiful with the hundreds of roses in arrangements everywhere. Incredible how the Road with the Roses had turned into the room full of roses! (More than two thousand roses for our wedding came direct from a rose farm in South America.)

Surprises awaited us at every turn. Mark called in so many favors, presenting us and our guests with special performances from a Cirque du Soleil artist, Broadway singers, and other fun moments of tribute from friends.

I had suggested somewhere in the evening we transition from a wedding party to a Christmas party, so sure enough, as Ron and I went on stage to cut the cake, we did not know that behind us the curtain was opening up to the most exquisite Christmas stage imaginable.

Three chefs stood in a row, ready to serve cake. A chocolate fountain with masses of fruit, as well as beautiful velvet couches, were next to the huge Christmas tree.

As we were cutting the cake we heard people whispering and gasping as the stage behind us came into view. Unaware of the curtain going up, I thought, "Hmmm, they must really be hungry for cake!" but, of course, they were in awe of Mark's handiwork on the stage. Everyone was invited up on stage to enjoy this Christmas finale, culminating with all of us singing "All of Me" with the piano.

It was nearly midnight when we said our good-byes to family, friends, and our four sons, reveling in all the richness. Tired but full in our hearts, we headed to our beautiful room upstairs.

I had been dreaming of my wedding night for years (talk about "glorious expectation!"). I was not disappointed.

CONSIDER THESE QUESTIONS

Do you believe Lynette's story is rare and only for a handful of people, or do certain choices make it possible for anyone to have exceedingly, abundantly more than they would ask or imagine?

Epilogue

The honeymoon was perfect in every way. Ron had arranged every detail of our two weeks together in the Caribbean. What a gift it was and so necessary for resting, having fun, and getting ready for a new set of adjustments ahead.

Returning to Raleigh, we were excited to see the boys and grateful to have a home already decorated for Christmas. The holidays would have awkward moments that first year, but over time our family has been knit together in deeply bonding ways.

Kim Ford, one of my best friends, is also a stepmom. She assured me that as time progresses you feel the same depth of love for your stepchildren as you do your own biological children. Her encouragement has proven so true.

From our wedding day forward, I have absolutely loved being married and still feel like a newlywed. But a month or two after the honeymoon, I awoke one morning thinking, "Hmmm, so this is it?"

Certainly there was no disappointment, but it was a bit surprising how similar the days after the wedding felt to those before. I still needed my own walk with God and was pursuing my dreams and aspirations, many of which now included Ron and the boys -- but these were still mine to pray over and pursue.

How grateful I was to not have placed everything on hold while waiting for marriage. If I had, there might be a sense of disappointment, a letdown of sorts.

Instead, the years of waiting had brought lessons that were actually gifts – gifts so hard to recognize in the midst of trials and pain. In these moments, if we can draw upon someone else's experiences, we feel less alone or crazy. We recognize that a larger plan is in motion, one entrusted to us, one calling us to hold out and believe.

On the pages that follow I share some of these lessons and gifts in the hope that you, too, will find courage as you persevere.

Section II

Gifts and Lessons
from the Journey

Every life journey is wrought with gifts, regardless of mistakes we make, wrongs done *to* us or *through* us. Oftentimes the gifts go unrecognized for years and only become clear through the lens of hindsight.

Reflecting on my journey, I am compelled to highlight some of these gifts in hope that you might recognize them in your own life, too, or go searching for those you have yet to see.

The Gift of Personal Wholeness

Next to the knowledge of Jesus Christ as Lord, the gift of personal wholeness runs a close second in its impact and influence on life. Personal wholeness is something that anyone can have; yet sadly, few do the work to get it.

Personal wholeness is crucial to living a fulfilled and happy life. It is what guides us into making life-giving choices, even when they are tough to make.

There are levels of wholeness that can perhaps be found apart from God, but to find wholeness in its fullest form requires a personal relationship with God. The Bible puts it: "You shall know the Truth and the Truth shall set you free." Only when we are walking in Truth (the way it really is) will we be free to come into the wholeness and healing we need.

In my book *Climbing the Ladder in Stilettos*, I devote Chapter 2 to this topic of wholeness. The definition I provide there is one I mention here again.

Being "whole" is defined as:

whole, adjective

1. complete, including all parts or aspects, with nothing left out

2. not damaged or broken

3. not wounded, impaired, or incapacitated

4. healed or restored to health physically or psychologically

Wholeness is a place we can get to in our soul and spirit where we are complete, secure, resilient.

> Only when we are walking in Truth (the way it really is) will we be free to come into the wholeness and healing we need.

During my college years when I felt the tremendous anxiety building, then went to counseling to get at the root of the pain, I started coming to new places of wholeness. Identifying pain-points which stemmed in large part from searching for my dad's approval was the first step toward wholeness.

Had I not found this wholeness, like so many I would have gone searching for a man to fill that void -- someone, anyone to say I am worthy, beautiful, and desirable. Looking to a human being leaves us broken, disappointed, and unsatisfied. Fortunately, I chose to develop a relationship with God instead.

Personal wholeness started coming to my heart and soul, a wholeness that could lead to wise choices in regards to men. These choices helped me not compromise or settle, saying no to versions of counterfeit love and waiting for healthy love from the man I would eventually marry.

I have a friend whose brother began messing around with her sexually at a very young age. Some might say (including her brother) it was all just innocent sibling exploration, but the truth is it ushered brokenness into both their lives.

These activities aroused sexual appetites in my friend at too young of an age. As a result, she became sexually active in her early teens and used sex to try to create intimacy with men. It was intimacy she needed but had never known with her father, brothers, or any men for that matter. The need was legitimate but the means to meet it was distorted, resulting in brokenness.

Her brokenness plunged her into a cycle of accepting sexual intercourse as a substitute for true intimacy, and now in her mid-thirties, growing in her walk with God, she is realizing that this brokenness has kept her in a cycle of dysfunction and disappointment.

My friend wants a healthy marriage with a man who loves her for more than her body, yet finding this will demand a process of healing that is crucial to her ultimate wholeness. Through counseling and an intense healing ministry called Cleansing Streams, my friend is coming into wholeness. For the first time she can envision waiting for sexual union to confirm, rather than attempting to create, lasting intimacy with a man.

Every human heart is made for this kind of intimacy. In a world that has cheapened sex and tries in every kinky way to get to new highs, my friend shines as a bright example of hope for something better.

> Had I not found this wholeness, like so many I would have gone searching for a man to fill that void.

The ability to wait and persevere comes from personal wholeness. As a person whose soul is intact and not broken, you can recognize and avoid anyone less than ideal or someone who would potentially lead to compromise.

When describing the way so many broken people approach relationships, I often use this example. A person comes to the table with a plate having only a saltine cracker and maybe an olive or two.

There they sit, hungry and hopeful that whoever sits across from them will have a plate with food to share. Instead, they attract another longing soul with a similar sparse plate. They both sit hungry, wanting to sample from the other's plate, hoping to somehow get filled, yet walking away as starved as when they arrived.

In contrast, two whole people come to the table with full plates, spread with all kinds of delicious delights. They can share liberally without the fear of coming up short, enjoying the delicacies each has to offer. At the end of every meal they are full and satisfied, with plenty left over for others beyond themselves.

Ron and I came to our relationship relatively whole and healed, in spite of what we had endured and the brokenness we had experienced. As we have combined our "full plates," we can feed hundreds, if not thousands, more.

A young man was recently explaining why he moved in with his girlfriend. He talked about how much it meant to him that she would move to the big city to be with him. As he shared it became clear that, like so many couples living together, there are bigger issues of brokenness going on in these two lives.

> The ability to wait and persevere comes from personal wholeness.

He is afraid of being rejected. She is desperate for male love and acceptance. Rather than becoming personally whole on their own, or making a real, formalized commitment that calls both of them to excellence, they invest just enough to stay together, hoping over time they will "feel ready" for marriage. Sadly, one dysfunction leads to another, and crippled people stay together, hoping to finish a marathon.

Over and over these less-than-best setups occur in a culture that applauds such arrangements and tells the rest of us we are old-fashioned to choose otherwise. Men treat women like rental cars, paying enough to keep driving, but not enough to buy. Women accept these terms without realizing they are worth far more than rent money. Both settle for less than the best, content to live broken lives versus finding deeper healing that sets them free to have it all.

If you are alone now, then do whatever it takes to get healthy inside and out. Becoming whole can feel at times like surgery. It is costly, messy, painful, and takes time to heal from the ache that comes from opening up the source of the wound and digging out the core of what is causing the pain inside.

But after a successful "surgery" (surgery may come in the form of counseling or various methods of prayer and ministry), you will indeed heal, and after you are whole, whatever was causing the ongoing pain is now but a distant memory. Many times it becomes a catalyst for offering help and wholeness to others afflicted with similar pain.

If you are currently in a relationship, you may need to take some time apart and individually come to a place of wholeness. If you are in a permanent relationship, you can still work on your own issues and the relationship will reap great benefits because of it.

Single or married, wholeness is something we must come to on our own; no one else can do it for us. Many a man or woman has stayed in a relationship with a broken individual just hoping against hope that a miracle will happen, praying their love interest will get over his anger, move past her pain, overcome bad habits that stem from brokenness.

> Over and over these less-than-best setups occur in a culture that applauds such arrangements and tells the rest of us we are old-fashioned to choose otherwise.

I have done this myself and look back with even firmer conviction that the best thing to do for a broken person is let them go and find their wholeness apart from you. Freeing them is the best way to expedite healing. We can stay nearby in some cases, continue praying and supporting, though in romantic relationships I do not recommend this. A clean break with no contact is usually the better method until wholeness comes and is obvious and consistent.

We all want to think our situation is unique and different, but rarely it is. Brokenness and its effects are almost universally the same -- destructive to a relationship and complicating to the point of failure. You do not need or want this!

My parents have been offering marriage counseling for almost 20 years, and they say that whatever issues you see in a dating relationship, double them and decide if you can live with that level of intensity, because that is how it will feel in marriage.

> Many a man or woman has stayed in a relationship with a broken individual just hoping against hope that a miracle will happen.

It is so true that marriage intensifies everything, good and bad. As my dear friend Toni puts it, "Marriage multiplies the state in which it finds you." If you're happy and whole as a single, then you will be even happier married. If you are broken and unhappy as a single, you will be even more unhappy once married. I have seen this truth play out in hundreds of friends through the years and now in my own life as well.

Marriage is a marathon, a long race requiring unique skills and training. Most people can go out and run a mile or two without much effort. But running 26.2 miles is different. Everyone at the start looks ready, decked out in the right clothes, excited to be running. But as the miles progress, only those trained and prepared have any hope of finishing.

Personal wholeness is a gift *everyone* can come to and enjoy. Use your single years to run after it and embrace it. Not only will it help you stay the course and wait for God's best, it will bring such a depth of enjoyment and satisfaction that the desire for marriage will take its healthy place in the mix of many other necessary and appropriate dreams.

Speaking of dreams, here is another gift worth pursuing.

CONSIDER THESE QUESTIONS

Relative to relationships, what are the signs that indicate someone is "whole"?

How "personally whole" do you believe you are right now in your life?

What are the most effective steps for someone to take to become whole?

Have you ever been close to someone who is broken? How did that affect you?

The Gift of Dreaming Big
for Your Life

While this story has focused on my dream of being married and having a family, I have had many other dreams as well. Dreams for my career, friendships, travel, my home, my wardrobe—all have been heart's desires for years.

When one dream is unrealized, the tendency is to focus all our energy, prayers, and attention on that one dream. We buy into the misconception, often subconsciously, that if only that dream were realized, then life would be great, or at least a lot better than it is now. In the intense process of waiting and wishing for that dream to come to pass, we easily miss gifts to be enjoyed via other dreams.

One thing I recognized as I waited to meet my husband was that life was moving along and time was passing by at an accelerated pace. As the saying goes, "Days are long but life is short."

I came to realize I had been given so many other worthwhile opportunities to live full and fulfilled. The challenge was to determine, over and over again, not to miss out on the present joys while waiting for those yet to come.

Many people ask, "How do I keep living when what I want so desperately is not happening?" My advice is always the same. Go for every other dream in your heart. Live those dreams; run after the ones you can pursue without restraint. Take whatever is in your present "field" and work that field with diligence and joy, drinking in every gift that goes with it.

> The challenge was to determine, over and over again, not to miss out on the present joys while waiting for those yet to come.

Heeding this advice myself meant embracing travel opportunities with work. I would invite Mom to go along many times to enjoy shows and shopping in New York or a fun women's retreat in Ohio. Other times I would connect with friends and tour Carmel, California, or spots in Florida.

One of my favorite stories illustrating this principle of living with the cup half full versus half empty, is that of Anne Frank, who from age 13 to 15 lived in hiding in Amsterdam to avoid Nazi captivity.

In that time she wrote short stories, essays, fairy tales, and the beginnings of a novel. Though she was in desperate need of deliverance and freedom, it did not keep her from exploring her dream of being a writer. Her journal, *The Diary of a Young Girl*, is a worldwide best seller many years following her death.

> Dreams are the energy of happiness. They help us stay focused beyond today's grind and envision possibilities that yet await.

I want to live like Anne did in her short fifteen-year life, never quitting what I call "dreaming on all cylinders." Dreams are the energy of happiness. They help us stay focused beyond today's grind and envision possibilities that yet await. Dreams ignite hope, pushing us outside our comfort zone, reminding us of our potential to do far more than we initially believe.

Besides the fulfillment and energy that pursuing dreams brings, it is also a very attractive quality, drawing like-minded fellow dreamers to us, and us to them.

One of the things that attracted Ron and I to each other is how we both love to dream big and then pursue those dreams, many of which, by God's grace, are helping us impact the world.

Ron would not have been attracted to someone sitting on the sidelines. Neither would I have wanted a forlorn, dejected man hoping someone would love him out of his broken state. The fact we were both achieving things in life, not content to rest on any laurels, was part of the magnetism that drew us together.

Living your dreams is a sure-fire way to meet the exact kind of people you want and need in your life, both as friends and as a potential life partner. While running your marathon you will notice the fellow runners able to keep up with your pace, striving for the same strong finish.

> Living your dreams is a sure-fire way to meet the exact kind of people you want and need in your life, both as friends and as a potential life partner.

Do whatever it takes to bring your dreams to life. Start purposefully and proactively pursuing at least one of them. This process of dreaming will so enliven and energize your heart that in no time at all you will be hooked forever on this "drug of dreaming" and be that much closer to living your dream life every day, even while a dream or two tarries.

CONSIDER THESE QUESTIONS

What are your three most prominent dreams in life right now?

How are you pursuing each of these?

What most keeps you from actively pursuing your dreams? How can you overcome these resistors?

What dreams would you like to see a man whom you're interested in, pursuing for his life?

The Gift of Sexual Energy

Our culture so romanticizes sexual love. Movies are filled with it, magazines talk about the latest techniques, entertainment programs highlight who is sleeping with who, and all with the underlying message: "Having sex is the ultimate high; you need and deserve it now!"

Personally, I'm a big fan of sex with my long-awaited husband, but it is just one component of a multidimensional relationship; important, yes, but not the end-all-be-all the culture says it is.

Frankly, sex is underrated...and also overrated, minimally it is misunderstood by a culture looking for True Love where it can't be found.

Empty people search for validation, treating sex as a means to get to know someone, the "hook-up" no different than meeting up for a drink. Sex becomes one more method for trying to *create* intimacy rather than *express* intimacy, and instead of being filled, those using it wrongly are left empty and disillusioned about what sex can and should be.

One friend confided this recently, opening up about how tired of the sex cycle she is at the age of 40, saying, "I now recognize most of my issues started with losing my virginity in my early teens."

Well-known pastor and wife, Mark and Grace Driscoll, put it this way: "...we have become utterly confused...people tend to think that sex is god or gross to varying degrees, rather than a gift."[5]

God commands, not suggests, that this gift belongs exclusively in marriage, because that is where it flourishes and thrives. Sadly, few in our culture, Christians or not, adhere to His design.

> Frankly, sex is underrated...and also overrated, minimally it is misunderstood by a culture looking for True Love where it can't be found.

In a sex-enamored world, taking a stand for sexual purity is a tough challenge. Even the phrase, "sexual purity," sounds old-fashioned and out of touch. One of my friends describes feeling like the odd woman out: "I remember being a virgin as a sorority girl in college, thinking I was really such a child and so alone. I was literally the only person I knew NOT sleeping around. Crazy."

Making this choice for sexual purity myself as a young girl, I had no idea it would require more than 30 years of commitment. I made a few mistakes along the way, but by the grace of God made it to the finish line, our wedding night. It *is* possible to walk in sexual purity, and yes, I would do it all over again.

You may relate more to my friend Lilly, who met her husband while dancing on a bar, literally *on* the bar. After just six weeks of dating they moved in together and later got married in Las Vegas. Their relationship began as she describes it, as "a train wreck waiting to happen," but over the years they met the Lord, got their issues dealt with, and today after 19 years of marriage have two adopted daughters and are leaders in the community and church.

Whether your story is like mine, Lilly's, or something in between, sexual purity is a gift worth pursuing, from a young age, or whatever age you are right now.

Sexual energy is God's idea. He gave it as a gift to Adam and Eve, saying, "Be fruitful and multiply." Sex is a powerful, multiplying force, two people coming together and multiplying—by having children and by being energized and fulfilled through their union.

So what do you do if you are not yet married and have this energetic force pulsating through your body?

As a passionate woman I developed passionate interests that offered creative outlets. One of them was cooking. I figured, "Hey, men love sex, but they also love to eat," so I started cooking up a storm!

I traveled, making the most of business trips to exciting cities. Being single is a perfect time to see the world, and I saw Italy, China, France, and dozens of American cities too, all on a shoe-string budget.

Now stick with me here. You may be thinking, "She's crazy! How can cooking or traveling take care of physical needs?"

> So what do you do if you are not yet married and have this energetic force pulsating through your body?

I appreciate the skepticism and wondered the same over the years, but the outlets I'm suggesting are minimally like taking a cold shower—or call them distractions from wasting physical investments for momentary thrills. My point is we do not have to sit in a corner wasting away in frustration. Let the energy flow, but find life-giving avenues versus dead-end streets.

Speaking of dead ends, we all fight the aging process, so being fit and exercising is another priority. I honed running skills, entered races, lifted weights. Working out is a great energy expender and yields benefits mentally and physically.

I love to decorate and spent years making curtains and pillows, turning small apartments into lovely homes. Mr. Right isn't likely to appreciate frills anyway, so go ahead and live it up now.

My professional life was an outlet, working hard, pouring hours and energy into projects, making career investments that a single life uniquely affords.

Always a bargain shopper, building a professional wardrobe provided an adventure in affordable, fashionable dressing. (I loved those 9 to 5 "dress-like-you-mean-it days.")

> People would sometimes ask when they found out I was a 40-year-old virgin, "Don't you feel like you're missing out?

Nonprofit organizations and ministry and church involvement brought great friends and the satisfaction of investing in others.

Best gift of all? Learning to pour my heart out to the Lord, discovering firsthand that intimacy with Him is the deepest satisfaction for every human heart. Years of singleness provided, if not forced, me to pursue Him with a vengeance, even though I wanted a human being to have and hold.

People would sometimes ask when they found out I was a 40-year-old virgin, "Don't you feel like you're missing out?" Well yes, I did -- missed out on heartache, regrets, recovery time, wondering time ("How much does he *really* like me?"), and the list goes on.

"Missing out" is all about perspective, and a lot of what I'm suggesting is about being wise and practical with our thought life and choices. If we choose a steady diet of *Sex and the City* and chick flicks showing everyone in bed, of course we feel left out, like we're the only one waiting.

If, on the other hand, we spend time with others standing for purity, and there are many, we feel normal, validated, and esteemed.

No matter what your sexual history, God has all the beauty and passion of lasting sexual intimacy planned for you. It is never too late to make healthy choices. You can even enjoy what is referred to as "secondary virginity," where your heart, mind, and thought life are restored and become like new.

Make no mistake about it; sexual purity is true sexual *freedom*. I say we start a revolution.

[5] Mark and Grace Driscoll, *Real Marriage* (Nashville: Thomas Nelson Inc., 2012), 110.

CONSIDER THESE QUESTIONS

We live in a "hook-up" culture where casual sex is like meeting for a drink. What value do you place on sex in a relationship? Should it be a means to intimacy or an expression of intimacy?

At what stage in a relationship should sex become a part? Have you ever considered saving sex for after marriage? Why or why not would this work for you?

How do you believe single guys honestly view women who have sex with them?

Are you happy with the sexual choices you've made thus far? Is your current view working for you (i.e. producing the outcomes you really want?)

Life Lessons

Not only has my journey yielded wonderful gifts, it has also taught several lessons worth sharing.

Know Your Life Purpose and Pursue It

For many years I have been leading workshops and speaking frequently on the topic of purpose. Rick Warren's book, *The Purpose-Driven Life* is the most famous on the subject and is a great read. Long before it was published, I was writing and speaking on this topic in many outlets.

The cry of every human heart is to know why we are here on this earth, the reason for our existence. (I devote Chapter 1 in *Climbing the Ladder in Stilettos* to this concept, complete with tools to uncover your purpose and write a purpose statement, along with ideas for living it every day.)

In the final episode of her long-running show, Oprah Winfrey put it like this, "Everybody has a calling, and your real job in life is to figure out what that is and get about the business of doing it."[6]

I will not go into great detail here on what purpose is and how to find it but will mention with great conviction that knowing your purpose is essential and lays the most solid foundation possible in the search for a life mate.

> The cry of every human heart is to know why we are here on this earth, the reason for our existence.

Purpose answers the question, "Why?" Why am I here? Why does my life matter? Sadly, too many people focus on the "What" (their mission, what they will do) and the "Who" (who I will date/marry, and who will be my friends). Before knowing what to do and who to do it with, we first need to know why.

For example, if my purpose is "to inspire and motivate people to know their purpose and live their dreams" (my personal purpose statement), then I can better determine what kinds of jobs and endeavors will best complement this purpose. It also helps filter the types of people who best align with this purpose as well as those who do not.

The more in touch you are with your life purpose before dating and marrying, the more quickly you can determine whether or not the two of you are a fit. Many a wrong combination could be avoided in business and in personal life if the parties involved would start by asking each other a set of "why" questions, the answers to which unlock the overriding purpose of why they are here and whether or not they belong together.

It is impossible here to cover all the ins and outs of "purpose," but suffice it to say that falling in love is not the hard part; staying married with differing purposes may be. Life purposes do not have to be identical for a lasting combination, but ideally they should be complementary. When they are, and both people are in tune with themselves on this level, they will enjoy many great advantages in facing life's inevitable ups and downs.

For anyone already married, you can find beautiful ways to blend even the most divergent of purposes. My encouragement here is for those not yet married, who will do well to focus on purpose now versus spending lots of energy and resources later, trying to make it work.

---

6 "The Oprah Winfrey Show Finale." The Oprah Winfrey Show. Prod. Harpo Productions Inc. ABC. WABC, New York. 25 May 2011.

CONSIDER THESE QUESTIONS

Do you believe you have a strong grip on your life purpose? If so, what is it, if not, would you like to have more clarity?

What role should personal purpose play in a relationship?

Cultivate a Vision of the Best

Maybe you have heard of people who make a list of the qualities they desire in a mate. I was one of them. My list began early, probably around the age of 15 or 16. Perhaps it was a friend who suggested I do so, or a mentor or book that prompted the first list. I wrote down in my journal the characteristics I desired, praying over them many times.

The list is about having specific standards and characteristics you want in a life partner before the person shows up in your life. Over the years my list changed; if anything, it grew to include more qualities I desired in a husband. While many are tempted to compromise and become more "open" with age, I became more specific, as my own personality and purpose were defined over the years.

Sadly, many people spend more time researching the car they want or the college they will attend than they do the person they will marry. Dating often becomes an experiment, something casually entered into while we wait to see if "it just feels right" and if so, we stay in; if not, we get out (or hopefully we do).

Imagine if one of the great researchers of our time was given a grant of a million dollars to find a cure for a dreaded disease. He must be clear on his objectives before ever qualifying for the money. He must also know what a cure looks like so his experiment has specific outcomes in mind.

If we simply approach dating as an experiment, not knowing what the ideal end result should look like, then we end up wasting something worth a whole lot more than a million dollars. We waste time, heart, emotions, and often our body. If we had only spent time with God, discovering His desires for our marriage, understanding those qualities He wants us to have in a mate, dating would become much simpler and so much more rewarding.

People often write me asking for help in finding a job. My response is always the same. I start by asking, "What kind of job do you want? What companies appeal to you? What type of people do you want to work with? What industries are you drawn to? Given your experience, what qualifies you for a certain job?" I ask these questions because they need a goal in mind, a target they want to reach. I, in turn, need more specificity in order to offer legitimate help.

> The Lord would often impress upon me, "If you get to know your husband in your prayer closet, you will know him when he shows up!

Choosing a spouse for life is far more important than a job search. During my years of waiting, the Lord would often impress upon me, "If you get to know your husband in your prayer closet, you will know him when he shows up!"

Prayer is so important, but so is being practical. One of the best books on this process of finding a mate is written by Neil Clark Warren, the founder of E-Harmony. *In Two Dates or Less, How to Know if Someone is Worth Pursuing* offers many "compatibility factors" useful in identifying a potential spouse. This can help you more quickly eliminate anyone with less compatible qualities. It is concrete knowledge that can greatly simplify the dating process – a process that often feels so complicated.

At the same time, these discoveries may lead to a feeling that no viable prospects exist. As my own list grew, so often did discouragement. Looking around I saw few, if any, who came close to fitting the list. As I shared earlier, Ron himself wondered if he might "fit the list."

I learned over time to be OK with this feeling. When I saw desirable qualities in those already married or in men I was drawn to as just friends, rather than focusing on the frustration, I chose to be grateful instead, grateful that the characteristics did exist, knowing God could pull them all together in one man who was right for me.

That he did! Ron possesses not only those qualities on my list, but many more. His "packaging" may be different than what I thought, but it is also better than what I expected.

God knows your needs and desires, and He answers prayer.

CONSIDER THESE QUESTIONS

What qualities and characteristics represent the ideal person for you?

How have these attributes guided your choices in dating and relationships, if at all?

Have you ever "settled" for something less than your best vision? Why or why not?

Pursue Deep, Meaningful Friendships

People are always the gift, and nowhere is this truer than in the journey of waiting for the man of your dreams. Throughout my years of waiting, so many wonderful friendships were the "fuel of endurance." Life is not meant to be lived alone, in spite of the fact that the testing of a dream can make us want to run away and hide, emerging only when it is over.

Meaningful friendships with both men and women keep the journey interesting, rewarding, and full of adventure. From the hundreds of ORU friends, to the Pete and Mary Kay Bible study group, to my sister, parents, bridesmaids, and church families, all were gifts sent to help bear burdens and not let me quit.

Sure, I was waiting for that friend of all friends in a husband, but even now I realize the very real need for other friends, those who add dimension and joy to so many aspects of life.

Personal wholeness, which I describe earlier, is an essential ingredient for healthy friendships. You can only give out of the overflow coming from your own life of wholeness. You may be the type who needs only a handful of close friends, or, like me, you may enjoy lots of different people in cities around the world.

Either way, cultivate healthy friendships that call you into a higher place of excellence, courage, and hope. Steer clear of those who cast doubt and unbelief when you express your dreams. No need to reject them, but it is crucial to depend on those with the capacity to comfort your heartaches and keep pointing to the promises of joy that will one day come.

> Cultivate healthy friendships that call you into a higher place of excellence, courage, and hope.

Friends like these watch over and care for our dreams like their own. When fulfillment comes, they share in the celebration.

One of my favorite parts of the show *American Idol* is early in the season when auditions take place around the country. While brave souls perform in front of the judges, friends and family wait outside to see if contestants will win the coveted yellow ticket to Hollywood for the next round. I love watching these friends scream and go nuts when those who are auditioning emerge with a yellow ticket. The friends respond as if they themselves are winning, and in a sense, they are.

Your dreams are not just about you, they connect you to indispensable friends running the race too.

I always enjoy going out to the New York City Marathon and watching as runners come through Central Park, just yards from the finish line.

The first year I watched, I remember thinking it odd that several of the runners had written their names large on the front of their t-shirts. "I'd never do that," I thought to myself. "How funky and self-promoting."

In that moment I heard a woman next to me shout, "Go Jerry, you are looking good. Keep it up, you're almost done!" There was

Jerry, bold-lettered name on his shirt, picking up more steam with a final burst of energy to make it to the finish line.

Then, I got it. When Jerry got up that morning he knew he would need people along the race route calling his name. People shouting, "Jerry, you look strong," assuring him he could finish. Rather than be too proud to let his weakness known, Jerry put his name out there, saying, in essence, "Help me run."

Reflecting on this experience a week or so later during my own run in Central Park, I was reminded of the Hebrews 11 passage, often called the "Hall of Faith." It describes so many great men and women who endured unbelievable trials in their journeys of faith.

Hebrews 12:1 says, "Therefore, since we are surrounded by such a great cloud of witnesses, let us throw off everything that hinders and the sin that so easily entangles, and let us run with perseverance the race marked out for us."

There running in Central Park, it was as if I could see these great people of faith looking down upon my running, just like I had done days before at the marathon.

I could almost hear their voices calling out my name, saying, "Lynette, we did it and so can you. We held on and kept believing, trusted God and saw Him come through. You can do it. Don't quit. Keep running. You are looking good, dear one, and we are cheering for you!"

I was so deeply encouraged and have gone back to that moment time and again. This is what friends are for! They line up on the sides of our roads, offer cups of water, an encouraging word, and strength when we are weary. They assure us that the finish line, though it feels so far in the distance, is just around the bend.

I used to think, "Some day my eclectic husband will take me

to great restaurants, to Broadway shows and the ballet, and we will explore New York City together on Saturdays from dawn to dusk." Truth is, while Ron and I do enjoy these things, it is rare, given our busy lives.

Fortunately, I did not wait for marriage to get out and enjoy my hobbies. I chose to live it up with friends until Ron came. Even now, girlfriends enjoy the ballet a whole lot more than he does. They get into fine restaurants with enthusiasm and are energized by shopping much more than my sweet husband will ever be.

Friends get us through. Mine sent flowers on Valentines Day, included me with their children for birthday parties, and called for spontaneous movies on some of the loneliest nights. We have laughed together, cried together, hoped and dreamed and prayed together. I am rich beyond measure, not just because dreams have come true, but because trusted friends have proven true.

CONSIDER THESE QUESTIONS

How good are you at cultivating deep, meaningful friendships? Are you naturally better at male or female friendships? Why?

Are you happy with the number of friendships you currently have?

What have you found to be the best practical ways to find and cultivate strong friendships?

What about friendships with men? Are they easy to come by or just too complicated?

Should someone maintain opposite sex friendships after they're married?

How do female friends give to one another in ways a guy never can?

What would be 1 or 2 practical ways a friend could give to you in ways that would really mean something to you?

Celebrate Now

I am a big believer in what I call, "Celebrating Your Season." Just like every season in the year has special perks we enjoy—things like barbeques in the summer, or Christmas lights in the winter—the seasons in our lives offer unique perks as well.

In nature too, every season has special beauty -- beauty wonderfully expressed as bare landscapes of winter turn into budding trees of spring, followed by the warmth of summer, then the colors of magnificent fall.

Our lives are so much the same. The key to a life of joy is less about dreams fulfilled and more about drinking in the here and now. The journey is as much a part of a joyful life as is reaching the destination.

I learned this truth when my first book was published. Writing for months and months felt like intense labor, but in hindsight, each juncture was as rewarding as having the book in hand.

It is all too easy to long for our next season rather than enjoy surprise gifts that emerge along the way. When we do this, I believe we sadden God's heart.

Imagine how I would have felt that first Christmas with Ron and the boys, having spent time decking the halls of our home, making delicious food I hoped they would love, if one of them piped up complaining, wanting lemonade instead.

Now granted, we all like lemonade, but it is not associated with Christmas in our house. In December we choose whipped cream-laden cups of hot chocolate by the fire. Summer days will return soon enough, but in the meantime, we are drinking "chocolate love," and not asking for lemonade!

> The key to a life of joy is less about dreams fulfilled and more about drinking in the here and now.

Walking with God is not all that different. Whenever we complain about our current season, or fail to celebrate the gifts present now, we are expressing mistrust in God and His supreme love and goodness.

One way I celebrate my season is by making a practice of choosing joy each morning when I wake up. Some mornings this comes easy and I do feel joyful. Many mornings it does not. Regardless, I am committed to being a woman of joy and hope, regardless of how I feel or how things look.

Living like this is a discipline, in thought, choices, and actions. It is not much different than a fitness routine.

I rarely feel like devoting an hour to running, followed by 15 minutes of weight training. I do, however, choose to be healthy and give my body what it needs to stay fit and strong. The more time I analyze how I feel about it, the easier it is to make excuses for why tomorrow will be better than today for going on that run.

I have learned in the twenty-five-plus years of running, that if I follow Nike's rule and "Just do it," I feel great afterwards and appreciate the many health benefits that a nutrition and fitness routine bring.

Likewise, hope and joy are a choice, not a feeling. They require discipline.

Every season has its gifts and I do not want to miss any of them, do you? Determine in your heart, as I have had to do over and over, to keep dreaming every dream and to celebrate *now*.

> Hope and joy are a choice, not a feeling. They require discipline.

Rather than waiting for that one unfulfilled dream to come true, start living it up today.

CONSIDER THESE QUESTIONS

Are you someone that knows how to celebrate life on a regular basis?

How do you most enjoy celebrating?

What might you do to add a broader sense of celebration in your life?

Decide to Wait and Not Compromise

I mentioned earlier how much I detest waiting. I know from many who write to me that I am not alone. Waiting is not for the faint of heart and requires several important skills if we are to hold out, hang on, and realize our dreams.

Taking the previous lessons to heart will help with the waiting. For instance, if I am a whole person who knows my purpose and understands the kind of mate I am waiting for, it is easier to wait until he comes, even if it takes longer than I hoped.

Imagine a father telling his 16-year-old daughter he is going to give her a new car. He does not specify *when* she will get it, but he does take her by the car lot to get a picture of the one he has in mind.

The daughter is so excited about her new car and figures any day now her father will bring it home. Months go by and she begins to wonder if he really meant what he said, but she looks at her three older brothers and sees how her father kept his word to them.

Her vision of what she knows is coming, along with the

faithfulness she knows to be true of her father, helps her endure and not go looking for any old junker she can afford at the time.

Waiting can bring on a sense of despair and hopelessness. We question whether or not we ever really heard from God. Is He faithful? Does He really care? Is He listening? What on earth is taking so long?

These are times when all the encouragement in the world may not seem to help. But then a ray of sunshine will somehow emerge in various ways, sometimes supernaturally, and we are able to wait again with more hope. The process is such a mystery and I wish there was more of a formula. Having a strong picture in our minds of the greatness we are holding out for, helps.

> In many ways it is about measuring success with a new measuring stick. If success is having a guy now and sex frequently, then those outcomes become our end goal.

In many ways it is about measuring success with a new measuring stick. If success is having a guy now and sex frequently, then those outcomes become our end goal.

If, on the other hand, our measure of success goes deeper, on levels not visible outwardly but lasting inwardly, then we have standards that help us wait, standards such as: Someone to love me always, and sex as an expression of intimacy versus an attempted means to find it.

Knowing the difference between counterfeits and the real thing is another tool for waiting. Professionals trained at recognizing counterfeit money learn this skill by studying the real thing. They are so in tune with the attributes of a real dollar bill, they can easily spot a fake.

In NYC you are never far from a knock-off district where fake bags abound. I have nothing against those who shop in that district, but it simply not work for me. There was a day when I thought those were a ould afford. I bought the bag and it looked good until it fell apart and I threw it away.

At this stage in my life, I prefer designer bags. Not because I need the external affirmations a brand-name purse might bring. For me, the quality and excellence reflect who I am.

Walking past the cheap bags takes guts. So many salespeople stand where the masses are, telling us to buy cheap because we absolutely must have a purse on our arm now.

I choose instead to sacrifice and save. Then, knowing I can afford a first-class bag, I can walk past the knock-offs and browse the designer selections.

In these shops the service is excellent; the surroundings are beautiful. I select the purse I love most and then, because I paid a high price, I treat it well, never feeling embarrassed or disappointed when carrying it with pride. Mine is not an arrogant pride with attitude, but a healthy pride with *gratitude*.

> I choose instead to sacrifice and save. Then, knowing I can afford a first-class bag, I can walk past the knock-offs and browse the designer selections.

I think you get the analogy here. This is how I feel being married to my husband, the man I saved up for, the one that required a designer price to pay, and one who, every day of our lives together, reassures me it was worth it.

Amidst a culture that tells us otherwise, we must become whole, trained, living on purpose, surrounded by like-minded friends, unwilling to settle for counterfeits, even when such a lifestyle looks crazy to the masses.

Keeping your heart pliable and honest before God, guarding against seeds of resentment and choosing to never compromise, will help you make it to your dream in a glorious way, deepening and growing as you wait for the real thing.

CONSIDER THESE QUESTIONS

Are you generally a patient or impatient person?

Do you feel behind, right on time, or ahead of the timeline you have had in mind relative to relationships?

What practical strategies might help you wait and hold out for the best?

Reflections on Truth

The following section includes many of the thoughts, reflections, and Scriptures written in my journals through the years of waiting and believing for dreams to come true. I have learned that for every emotion I experience, God has something powerful to say about Himself and His provision.

During our struggles, it is vital to meditate on His Truth, acknowledging our feelings and being honest, then moving through those emotions to a place of trust in Him.

One powerful way to do this is by finding out what He has to say about what we are feeling and experiencing. The Word of God is relatable to all of our deepest questions and pain. It is ultimate Truth, the way it really is.

As you meditate on Truth, I hope these reflections will help carry and lift you to new hope and confidence as you, too, wait on Him.

FOR DISCUSSION RELATIVE TO EACH JOURNAL
ENTRY THAT FOLLOWS, DISCUSS WAYS TO
ADDRESS THESE EMOTIONS CONSTRUCTIVELY,
ENCOURAGING HONESTY AND UNDERSTANDING OF
WHOLENESS RELATIVE TO EACH EMOTION.

Hopeless

Oh Lord, I feel as if all my hope is gone. How can I possibly muster up more hope when for so long all I've hoped for has consistently been denied? You say in Proverbs 13:12, "Hope deferred makes the heart sick..." and so it is with me, I feel sick. I'm sick and tired of this endless cycle of my hopes being stirred and then later dashed. I need new hope, new courage, Lord. Only you can give me what I need. Teach me how to hope in spite of circumstances, in spite of how I feel or the way things look. Lord, I look to You and You alone. I want to be a woman of hope but right now I am utterly hopeless.

The Truth

Job 6:8, 11-13 Oh, that I might have my request, that God would grant what I hope for...vs. 11 What strength do I have, that I should still hope? What prospects, that I should be patient? Do I have the strength of stone? Is my flesh bronze? Do I have any power to help myself, now that success has been driven from me?

Job 13:15-16 Though he slay me, yet will I hope in him; I will surely defend my ways to his face. Indeed, this will turn out for my deliverance...

Psalm 25:3-5 No one whose hope is in you will ever be put to shame, but they will be put to shame who are treacherous without excuse. Show me your ways, O LORD, teach me your paths; guide me in your truth and teach me, for you are God my Savior, and my hope is in you all day long.

Proverbs 13:4 The sluggard craves and gets nothing, but the desires of the diligent are fully satisfied.

Stifled and Squelched

Lord, you have made me full of passion and creativity, with so much energy I long to pour out to the one I love. What can I do with this passion? I feel so squelched and stifled, as if I'm a pot of boiling water with the lid on top, one that if left alone will simply boil over for no good. What am I to do with all this energy and passion inside? If I hold back I'm frustrated and even more desperate, yet if I pour it out in a wrong direction I'm filled with regret and disappointment. I feel trapped Lord, like I can't win either way. You are the one who has given me all this energy and passion, where shall I direct it and how can I flow in a way that is productive and honors you?

The Truth

Isaiah 54:2-5 Enlarge the place of your tent, stretch your tent curtains wide, do not hold back; lengthen your cords, strengthen your stakes. For you will spread out to the right and to the left; your descendants will dispossess nations and settle in their desolate cities. Do not be afraid; you will not suffer shame. Do not fear disgrace; you will not be humiliated. You will forget the shame of your youth and remember no more the reproach of your widowhood. For your Maker is your husband – the Lord Almighty is his name – the Holy One of Israel is your Redeemer; he is called the God of all the earth.

Jeremiah 20:9 But if I say, "I will not mention him or speak any more in his name," his word is in my heart like a fire, a fire shut up in my bones. I am weary of holding it in; indeed, I cannot.

Isaiah 58:10-11 And if you spend yourselves in behalf of the hungry and satisfy the needs of the oppressed, then your light will rise in the darkness, and your night will become like the noonday. The LORD will guide you always; he will satisfy your needs in a sun-scorched land and will strengthen your frame. You will be like a well-watered garden, like a spring whose waters never fail.

Tired and Weary from the Wait

I feel as if I am spent, like all my strength is gone and I'm unable to sustain this journey. I want to be full of energy, excited about life, able to finish this race with flying colors. It takes strength to just keep on walking, waiting, strength that is non-existent right now. People ask me, "What's wrong?" I don't want to tell them, "It's because I'm waiting for a husband." That seems so desperate and shortsighted, yet it is so true. There has got to be a way to be energized. Will I have to wait much longer? The thought of this puts me completely over the edge. How can I continue for weeks, months, years, and not bail out completely and compromise?

The Truth

Psalm 27:14 Wait for the Lord; be strong and take heart and wait for the LORD.

Psalm 33:20 We wait in hope for the LORD; he is our help and our shield.

Psalm 37:7-9 Be still before the LORD and wait patiently for him; do not fret when men succeed in their ways, when they carry out their wicked schemes. Refrain from anger and turn from wrath; do not fret – it leads only to evil. For evil men will be cut off, but those who hope in the LORD will inherit the land.

Isaiah 40:28-31 Do you not know? Have you not heard? The LORD is the everlasting God, the Creator of the ends of the earth. He will not grow tired or weary, and his understanding no one can fathom. He gives strength to the weary and increases the power of the weak. Even youths grow tired and weary and young men stumble and fall; but those who hope in the LORD will renew their strength. They will soar on wings like eagles; they will run and not grow weary, they will walk and not be faint.

Lamentations 3:24 I say to myself, "The LORD is my portion; therefore I will wait for him."

Ugly and Unattractive

Maybe I'm just not beautiful enough to attract someone. I know beauty comes from within but I don't get much attention these days. It's hard to stay motivated to be in shape and in style when no one seems to notice or care. I want someone to be drawn to my heart, my mind, and yes my body too, but what is the balance? How much does external beauty matter in catching the eye of the one you have for me? Lord, teach me what true beauty is, help me understand health and nutrition in order to be physically fit, but in a balanced way so I don't obsess. Let me radiate your true, lasting beauty, inside and out. May it be your Holy Spirit that draws the man of your choosing.

The Truth

1 Peter 3:3-4 Your beauty should not come from outward adornment, such as braided hair and the wearing of gold jewelry and fine clothes. Instead, it should be that of your inner self, the unfading beauty of a gentle and quiet spirit, which is of great worth in God's sight.

Proverbs 31: 30-31 Charm is deceptive, and beauty is fleeting; but a woman who fears the Lord is to be praised. Give her the reward she has earned, and let her works bring her praise at the city gate.

Song of Solomon 4:16 Awake, north wind, and come, south wind! Blow on my garden, that its fragrance may spread abroad. Let my lover come into his garden and taste its choice fruits.

Jealous

I look at my friends and many others enjoying dating, marriage, and children. I feel so jealous of what they have, and then I feel horrible about the jealousy. Lord, you say, "Thou shall not covet," yet I do covet, I want what they have. I have laid these desires on the altar so many times and yet how am I supposed to really let go of a heart's desire? I have so much to be grateful for, yet the things I desire most are consistently denied. Oh God, teach me how to celebrate the joy of my friends, I need so much grace Lord, grace to rejoice with those who rejoice. Let their answers encourage me as I wait. Instead of feeling jealous let me be invigorated knowing that what you do for others you can and will do for me. Rather than pulling away from them, let me move in and invest in their joy. I sow it as a seed unto you oh Lord, confident you will reward me a hundred-fold when my time comes. Oh God I so desperately need you. I want to run away and hide but with your help I will move in and share in their joy, trusting you for grace to be sincerely happy for them.

The Truth

Romans 12:15 Rejoice with those who rejoice; mourn with those who mourn.

2 Corinthians 9:6-8, 10-15 Remember this: Whoever sows sparingly will also reap sparingly, and whoever sows generously will also reap generously. Each man should give what he has decided in his heart to give, not reluctantly or under compulsion, for God loves a cheerful giver. And God is able to make all grace abound to you so that in all things at all times, having all that you need, you will abound in every good work. Now he who supplies seed to the sower and bread for food will also supply and increase your store of seed and will enlarge the harvest of your righteousness.

You will be made rich in every way so that you can be generous on every occasion, and through us your generosity will result in thanksgiving to God. This service that you perform is not only supplying the needs of God's people, but is also overflowing in many thanks to God. Because of the service by which you have proved yourselves, men will praise God for the obedience that accompanies your confession of the gospel of Christ and for your generosity in sharing with them and with everyone else. And in their prayers for you their hearts will go out to you, because of the surpassing grace God has given you. Thanks be to God for his indescribable gift!

Mad at God

I know it's so ridiculous and foolish to be mad at the God of the Universe, the One I believe has my best interest at heart, the One who so loves me beyond what I can imagine. Yet I feel so hurt and angry with you God. Why do you forsake me? Why do you stand so far off and seem so disinterested in my desires? Have I not been faithful? Have I not kept my end of the bargain? Bargain -- that sounds so trite and yet that's what I thought we had, a deal, an arrangement, that there would be a legitimate reward for my faithfulness, maybe not because I deserve it but because you are faithful and good. You supposedly love to grant the desires of your children. Doesn't a parent want their child to be happy and satisfied? Yet you deny me over and over, saying no to my choices, blinding the eyes of those whom I desire. What am I left with but to assume you don't care, that you are so busy answering the prayers of others that you haven't had time yet for me. I feel like I'm wrestling with you God, and that you always prevail. I feel trapped, like I can't win either way. On the one hand I only want what you want for my life, yet I cannot understand why you aren't answering. I could make something happen, manipulate circumstances and people to satisfy my cravings and desires, yet I know it would only leave me wanting and disappointed even more than I already am. So I'm stuck here waiting, waiting on your answers, answers that never come; having no answers of my own; seeing no point at all in this agony I must endure; feeling like you have abandoned me. How can I trust you when I see no sign of your attention?

The Truth

Psalm 10: 1 Why, O LORD, do you stand far off? Why do you hide yourself in times of trouble?

Psalm 22:1-5, 14 My God, my God, why have you forsaken me? Why are you so far from saving me, so far from the words of my groaning? O my God, I cry out by day, but you do not answer, by night, and am not silent. Yet you are enthroned as the Holy One, you are the praise of Israel. In you our fathers put their trust; they trusted and you delivered them. They cried to you and were saved; in you they trusted and were not disappointed. I am poured out like water and all my bones are out of joint. My heart has turned to wax, it has melted away within me.

Psalm 13 How long, O LORD? Will you forget me forever? How long will you hide your face from me? How long must I wrestle with my thoughts and every day have sorrow in my heart? How long will my enemy triumph over me? Look on me and answer, O LORD my God. Give light to my eyes, or I will sleep in death; my enemy will say, "I have overcome him," and my foes will rejoice when I fall. But I trust in your unfailing love, my heart rejoices in your salvation. I will sing to the Lord for he has been good to me.

Powerless

I am a make-it-happen woman; I go for the dreams in my heart, the aspirations of my life. I get frustrated with others who wait for some lottery to give them what they want or need. My philosophy is, "If you know what you desire then put together a strategy to go after it." But in this area of my life, desiring a husband and children, I cannot work the same way and get the results I want. I've tried taking matters fully in my own hands, listening to the well-meaning advice of those who say I need to do more, be more open, get out more frequently, quit waiting for the husband to just fall from the sky. Yet in this matter of a husband and children I really am totally and utterly dependent on you God. All my efforts have proven futile, leaving me only more frustrated and disappointed. It seems I am better off letting go altogether, being open yes, but living in the truth that You are sovereign, in charge, ordering my steps and the steps of my husband, to bring us together at the appointed time. I believe you are all-powerful and can creatively and ingeniously bring us together in your perfect way and timing. The Road with the Roses is longer than expected, at least the part where I walk alone. Keep my vision fixed on you, oh Lord. I'm bent on remembering that your power helps me put one foot in front of the other, and keep on walking.

The Truth

Jeremiah 32:17 Ah, Sovereign LORD, you have made the heavens and the earth by your great power and outstretched arm. Nothing is too hard for you.

1 Corinthians 4:7-12, 16-18 But we have this treasure in jars of clay to show that this all-surpassing power is from God and not from us. We are hard pressed on every side, but not crushed; perplexed, but not in despair; persecuted, but not abandoned; struck down, but not destroyed. We always carry around in our body the death of Jesus, so that the life of Jesus may also be revealed in our body. For we who are alive are always being given over to death for Jesus' sake, so that his life may also be revealed in our mortal body. So then, death is at work in us, but life is at work in you. Therefore we do not lose heart. Though outwardly we are wasting away, yet inwardly we are being renewed day by day. For our light and momentary troubles are achieving for us an eternal glory that far outweighs them all. So we fix our eyes not on what is seen, but on what is unseen, since what is seen is temporary, but what is unseen is eternal.

2 Corinthians 12:7-10 To keep me from becoming conceited because of these surpassingly great revelations, there was given me a thorn in my flesh, a messenger of Satan, to torment me. Three times I pleaded with the Lord to take it away from me. But he said to me, "My grace is sufficient for you, for my power is made perfect in weakness." Therefore I will boast all the more gladly about my weaknesses, so that Christ's power may rest on me. That is why, for Christ's sake, I delight in weaknesses, in insults, in hardships, in persecutions, in difficulties. For when I am weak, then I am strong.

Frustrated and Foolish

So here I am telling everyone for years, "God is faithful, He has a husband for me, I know he's coming, I'll wait as long as it takes." Talking like this is fine for a few years I suppose, but 15+ years God? I wonder if people don't just pity me behind their backs, think I should get a reality check and quit having such a fantasy. Sometimes I honestly wonder the same. It feels so awkward to be the only single one left in so many groups of friends. Even all my cousins on both sides, all younger than me, are all married now. I know my journey is unique, crafted with Your love and best interest for my life. But it's hard not to be embarrassed sometimes, saying the same things over and over whenever people ask why I'm still single, with no signs of any change.

The Truth

Psalm 66:10-12, 16-20 For you, O God, tested us; you refined us like silver. You brought us into prison and laid burdens on our backs. You let men ride over our heads; we went through fire and water, but you brought us to a place of abundance. Come and listen, all you who fear God; let me tell you what he has done for me. I cried out to him with my mouth; his praise was on my tongue. If I had cherished sin in my heart, the Lord would not have listened; but God has surely listened and heard my voice in prayer. Praise be to God, who has not rejected my prayer or withheld his love from me!

Psalm 68:4-7, 9-11 (AMP) Sing to God, sing praises to His name, cast up a highway for Him Who rides through the deserts – His name is the Lord – be in high spirits and glory before Him! A father of the fatherless and a judge and protector of the widows is God in His holy habitation. God places the solitary in families and gives the desolate a home in which to dwell; He leads the prisoners out to prosperity; but the rebellious dwell in a parched land. You, O God, did send a plentiful rain; You did restore and confirm Your heritage when it languished and was weary. Your flock found a dwelling place in it; You, O God, in Your goodness did provide for the poor and needy. The Lord gives the word (of power); the women who bear and publish (the news) are a great host.

Getting Too Old

I feel panicked, life used to seem so long with so many years to come. Now days feel like they're slipping away at lightning speed, and I'm falling so far behind. I've lived so much of the prime of life already. How will I not feel in later years, that my husband and I missed out on so much life together? Then there's my biological clock. I pray over my ovaries, "Oh God, keep them fresh and green and young!" But year after year I'm aging, with fertility looking more and more like a futile dream of the past. I used to wonder why women become desperate about their age. Now I understand, and I just can't believe I'm one of them. Even Hollywood produced a movie about me, "The 40-yr old Virgin!"

The Truth

Joshua 14:7-14 I was forty years old when Moses the servant of the LORD sent me from Kadesh Barnea to explore the land. And I brought him back a report according to my convictions, but my brothers who went up with me made the hearts of the people melt with fear. I, however, followed the LORD my God wholeheartedly. So on that day Moses swore to me, 'The land on which your feet have walked will be your inheritance and that of your children forever, because you have followed the LORD my God wholeheartedly. "Now then, just as the LORD promised, he has kept me alive for forty-five years since the time he said this to Moses, while Israel moved about in the desert. So here I am today, eighty-five years old! I am still as strong today as the day Moses sent me out; I'm just as vigorous to go out to battle now as I was then. Now give me this hill country that the LORD promised me that day. You yourself heard then that the Anakites were there and their cities were large and fortified, but, the LORD helping me, I will drive them out just as he said." Then Joshua blessed Caleb son of Jephunneh and gave him Hebron as his inheritance. So Hebron has belonged to Caleb son of Jephunneh the Kenizzite ever since, because he followed the LORD, the God of Israel, wholeheartedly.

Psalm 92:14 They will still bear fruit in old age, they will stay fresh and green.

Luke 1:36-37 (AMP) And listen! Your relative Elizabeth in her old age has also conceived a son, and this is now the sixth month with her who was called barren. For with God nothing is ever impossible and no word from God shall be without power or impossible of fulfillment. Then Mary said, Behold, I am the handmaiden of the Lord; let it be done to me according to what you have said.

Romans 4:18-21 Against all hope, Abraham in hope believed and so became the father of many nations, just as it had been said to him, "So shall your offspring be." Without weakening in his faith, he faced the fact that his body was as good as dead—since he was about a hundred years old—and that Sarah's womb was also dead. Yet he did not waver through unbelief regarding the promise of God, but was strengthened in his faith and gave glory to God, being fully persuaded that God had power to do what he had promised.

To Sum It All Up

"Maybe this happy ending doesn't include a wonderful guy, maybe it's you, on your own, picking up the pieces and starting over, freeing yourself up for something better in the future. Maybe the happy ending is just moving on. Or maybe the happy ending is this, knowing that through all the unreturned phone calls and broken hearts, through all the blunders and misread signals, through all the pain and embarrassment, you never, ever gave up hope."
Quote from Gigi (Ginnifer Goodwin)[7]
He's Just Not That Into You

What would have become of me had I not believed that I would see the Lord's goodness in the land of the living! Wait and hope for and expect the Lord; be brave and of good courage and let your heart be stout and enduring. Yes, wait for and hope for and expect the Lord.
Psalm 27:13-14 (AMP)

This vision-message is a witness pointing to what's coming. It aches for the coming - it can hardly wait! And it doesn't lie. If it seems slow in coming, wait. It's on its way. It will come right on time.
Habakkuk 2:3 (MSG)

[7] Kwapis, Ken, director, *He's Just Not That Into You.* Warner Brothers, 2009. DVD

Recommended Resources

Here are a few of my favorite books, those that were food for my soul on the Road with the Roses.

I Gave God Time by Ann Kiemel Anderson

Passion and Purity by Elisabeth Elliot

The Sacred Romance by John Eldredge

Journey of Desire by John Eldredge

Wild at Heart by John Eldredge

Captivating by John and Stasi Eldredge

Seductions Exposed: The Spiritual Dynamics of Relationships by Gary L. Greenwald

You Gotta Keep Dancin' by Tim Hansel

The Screwtape Letters by C.S. Lewis

Life of the Beloved: Spiritual Living in a Secular World by Henri J.M. Nouwen

When God Weeps: Why Our Sufferings Matter to the Almighty by Joni Eareckson Tada

Date or Soul Mate?: How to Know if Someone is Worth Pursuing in Two Dates or Less by Neil Clark Warren

Finding the Love of Your Life by Neil Clark Warren

The Triumphant Marriage by Neil Clark Warren

The Mystery of Marriage by Mike Mason

About the Author

For more information and resources from Lynette Lewis, or to share your own journey, insights, and questions, please visit LynetteLewis.com, and the Lynette Lewis Page on Facebook. You can also follow her on Twitter at Lynette_Lewis.

To book Lynette for a speaking engagement, please use the contact form on her website, or write to info@LynetteLewis.com.

Notes and Reflections